Frank Field has been the MP fo
chairs the Cathedrals Fabric Co
the author of a number of bo
Attlee's Great Contemporaries (20

SAINTS AND HEROES

Inspiring politics

Frank Field

To Sally Delafield Cook

First published in Great Britain in 2010

Society for Promoting Christian Knowledge
36 Causton Street
London SW1P 4ST

British Library Cataloguing-in-Publication Data
A catalogue record for this book is available from the British Library

ISBN 978–0–281–06187–7

1 3 5 7 9 10 8 6 4 2

Typeset by Graphicraft Limited, Hong Kong
Printed in Great Britain by Ashford Colour Press

Produced on paper from sustainable forests

Contents

————•◦•————

Preface   vii

Six heroes and one hymn sheet   1

Part 1
THE TEMPLE FAMILY

Introduction   15

1 Last of the great Victorians   17

2 Father and son: the relative abilities of
   Frederick and William Temple   21

3 William Temple's business ethics: stymieing
   the left for a generation   36

4 William Temple: a political evaluation   50

5 *Christianity and Social Order*: the book and
   the nation   62

Part 2
A MAGNIFICENT ACT

Introduction   79

6 George Bell: a uniquely consistent life   82

7 *Piety and Provocation: A study of George Bell*   98

8 Two heroes, one message   101

Contents

Part 3
MADAM INVINCIBLE

Introduction 113

9 Citizenship and the politics of behaviour:
   lessons from Eleanor Rathbone's thought 114

10 Looking back to greatness: 50 years on 131

11 The whisper of greatness 137

Part 4
LEADING THE MASTER CLASS

Introduction 145

12 Beveridge: in a league of his own 146

Notes 158

Preface

All but one of these essays were given as talks or lectures or written as reviews over the past 15 years or so. I have edited them into a book and added a new essay on William Beveridge. That there are no essays on any other of my heroes, such as R. H. Tawney and Clement Attlee, is partly because I have yet to be asked to speak on Tawney (a reflection of New Labour's lack of ideological roots, perhaps) and I have elsewhere used the opportunity of bringing together 30 of Attlee's reviews in *Attlee's Great Contemporaries* (London: Continuum, 2009) to set out my admiration for his character and dignified style of democratic leadership.

Jill Hendey, my secretary, transcribed the essays into publishable form, Damian Leeson read through the whole manuscript, questioned lines of thought and much sharpened up its presentation, and Ruth McCurry and Liz Jones have set exacting standards editing the text and making numerous helpful suggestions and additions. I am grateful for the efforts of all three individuals but I remain wholly responsible for the opinions, judgements and any errors that remain.

Six heroes and one hymn sheet

All six of my heroes had a view about what kind of leadership is necessary in a democracy. That leadership was in part provided by the character of those who aspired to high office. It also came from a group singing from the same hymn sheet, by which I mean that they all signed up to a public ideology built around the ideas and beliefs of English Idealism.

The public ideology of English Idealism

Some people may ponder whether Frederick Temple appears too early on the scene to have helped directly in the development of the English Idealist tradition that formed this near universally accepted public ideology, but he was very much part of what is called the broad church movement from which Idealism sprang. Frederick also helped foster an intellectual tradition that saw history teaching the great truths, and it was this insight that T. H. Green, the father of English Idealism, developed so effectively by using the 'eye of history' to reassert them.

Green's brilliance was manifest in a number of forms. He faced head-on the causes of the doubt beginning to undermine the intellectual hegemony that was such a measurable feature of British society up until the middle years of Victoria's reign. Part of Green's achievement was to separate the kernel of Christian belief, which had for well over 1,000 years acted as our public ideology, from an adherence to the literal truth of the Gospel miracles.

In one fell swoop he gained support from three disparate groups. There were those I might call the traditionalists, who were pleased to have an advocate who took their message on to the front foot once again.[1] Next was a grouping that felt the

1

game was up as far as orthodox Christianity went, unless its essence could be decanted into new bottles made in the age in which they lived; Green's explanation of Christianity allowed this group once again to hold up its head in a world of reason. Last came a group who believed Christianity could no longer be intellectually defended on any grounds, no matter how ingeniously conceived, but who wished to maintain most of Christian moral teaching without having this message ridiculed by what they saw as its Siamese twin of insupportable Christian dogma. Green's goal was to allow Christian ethics to be defended by reason alone.[2]

For a hundred years or so we were all beneficiaries of Green's brilliance. With little or no conscious effort on our part, most citizens knew what life's overall aim was – to achieve one's best self. They also knew that this goal could not be secured unless those people around us, and not only those whom we love, are similarly committed. All of my heroes from Frederick onwards carried out their public life without having to explain, let alone defend, these basic rules of the game. And this remained true irrespective of whether they were believers or agnostics.

The most religious of my heroes, William Temple, was as much a disciple of Green as were the sceptics like Eleanor Rathbone and William Beveridge. Temple's social programme owed everything to Green and to his interpretation of Christian social duties, and Temple's own social message gained only passing support from his carefully crafted religious philosophy. Eleanor Rathbone was schooled in Green as an Oxford undergraduate and lived out her life renewing Green's conception of an active citizenry. William Beveridge, similarly, came to his ideas of a self-governing citizenry partly by drawing on the civil republican tradition that bubbles along as part of our own political culture. Beveridge was a beneficiary of Green's actions, as the initiator of Idealism did much to encourage an overflowing of this republican tradition back into the mainstream of political thinking here in the UK.[3]

Our political agenda today is back to the one Frederick Temple carved out with such resolution and foresight. If our society is to resume its journey on the road to greater progress we have to regroup around Frederick's insight into education, namely that offering individuals a chance to fulfil their best selves also, crucially, offers the most secure way to advance society as a whole. There is, however, one crucial difference between Frederick's time and our own. While the Christian orthodoxy that Frederick espoused was safely refashioned into a public ideology of Idealism, we now live in a world where that tradition has ceased to be renewed in any meaningful and relevant way.

This agreement about objectives no longer exists in our society. The cutting edge of English Idealism has been replaced by a series of much softer stances centring around the goal of happiness and well-being. But these generalized expressions of intent provide no structure for our corporate lives. Nor are we given a necessary social compass for their implementation.

Britain now has no agreed public ideology. We have torn up the hymn sheet. The most dramatic reported example I have come across on how society has ceased to sing from the same hymn sheet was provided for me when I visited Australia, whose society faces the same fundamental weakness as we do. In October 2005, a Sydney magistrate dismissed a case brought against a youth who had drunkenly sworn obscenities at the police in a public street. Rubbing salt into the wound, she ordered the police to pay the offender's costs of $2,600. She told the court, 'I am not sure there is such a thing as community standards any more.'[4]

Here is another crucial difference between the world in which we live and that inhabited by my six heroes. Then it was not just the elite who shared an agreed hymn sheet. Practically all of us knew the tunes and were enthusiastic singers. Mr Attlee was the last prime minister who consciously thought of himself as belonging to the Idealist tradition, even if he had renounced Idealistic reasoning as no better than the mumbo-jumbo of Christianity, which he rejected so early on in his adult life.[5]

There are two significant changes between our own time and Frederick's. The first centres on how careless, not to say irresponsible, our own elite was during the second half of the last century in failing to renew the then existing social capital that carried the hallmark of English Idealism. The result was not immediately apparent as there was so much social capital to deplete. But this failure has ultimately left us without an agreed hymn sheet from which to sing out our private goals, proclaiming both what they are and the way they simultaneously parallel our objectives as social animals.

Britain urgently needs the 'conversion' experience which our Victorian forebears so willingly underwent as they fell in love with the best aspects of the Greek ideal of citizenship. To face the turmoil of the first rapidly industrializing society this elite looked back to an idealized Greek role model. To deliver a society that could safely embrace change without violently upsetting the established social order, our not too distant ancestors embraced and promoted that idealized conception of citizenship.

Their success was tangible. English Idealism breathed new life into that ancient concept and, in so doing, crafted a public ideology which gave individuals and groups a clear sense of what was expected of them. This ideology, governing so much of public conduct, gave what now appears to be an unimaginable degree of confidence to those whose role was initiating the young into the wider society. These foot-soldiers of any democratic society – the clergy, teachers, police, factory and health inspectors, doctors, voluntary workers and a growing host of other officials – went about their task with an easy assurance. While they attended directly to their profession – teaching or policing, for example – they also understood that their work fitted into a much larger picture. They were committed to this wider goal of improving the character they and their charges possessed. They also knew that if their decisions were disputed, they would be unquestionably backed by society's most influential members.

My heroes, despite their differing views on Christian belief, were all part of that great collective endeavour. So here, in this introductory chapter, I highlight those aspects of their public lives that were dedicated to this end and that I would have most liked to have expressed myself.

Frederick Temple

All six heroes had an important impact on this country as well as having an influence on me as a politician. Frederick Temple's appeal lies in being a classic Victorian hero. He rose from impoverished beginnings to the very apex of the Victorian social pyramid. It is a thrilling tale, devoid of any hint of the flashiness that now inevitably forms part of the celebrity wardrobe.

Frederick's meteoric rise was achieved against huge odds, and his unwillingness to trim or compromise his beliefs in any way, let alone to ingratiate himself to that class that would determine his advance, makes him all the more appealing to me. His willingness not to take prisoners as he advanced is the stuff of which story books are made. Yet his rise is also relevant to our own politics, where social immobility is becoming ever more rooted. What are the lessons for us in Frederick's rise?

Two characteristics stand out and serve as pointers to how we might act. The first is the role of his widowed mother who, while not herself educated, was both his early mentor and then the agent expelling Frederick and his siblings from the family's genteel poverty. How can we today find similar figures to carry out this mentoring role in the growing number of chaotic families where the parents are part of the problem, rather than the solution? Likewise, how do we best repair the damage to an educational system which was there to welcome Frederick and was similarly open to Frederick's best efforts to develop and improve its effectiveness? Anthony Crosland and Mrs Thatcher have much to answer for here, as one was the architect and the other the most significant acolyte in destroying the universality of grammar schools in this country.

Frederick stands apart from my other five heroes. The others, including his own son who benefited from Frederick's rapid social advance, come from privileged middle- or upper-middle-class backgrounds. It was not for them a question of making it, but rather of how they exercised their time as occupants in the top drawer of British society.

William Temple

While I warmed to the role Frederick's son William played in making Mr Attlee's great reforming government possible, William's greatest attraction for me lies in his single and out-standingly courageous act in what turned out to be the last stages of his life. William had lived most of that life in the mind, yet when events could no longer be understood within the framework through which he had always viewed the world, he was willing not only to ask but also to answer the most funda-mental questions about how God worked in the world.

Merely to write these words makes me want to shout my approval. Here was an uncharacteristically brave act by someone who had seen his own life thrive and prosper in the shade of the soft incarnational theology that had taken hold of Anglican thinking as his father mounted the steps to the throne of St Augustine in the last years of the nineteenth century. As World War II approached, William accepted that the way he had viewed the world was now fatally flawed. William's willingness, dare I say it, to think the unthinkable, and act, holds a special appeal for me.

George Bell

Bell's life, by contrast, offers the very different political lesson of how a single public act of extraordinary and indeed reckless courage and strategic importance can help renew a nation's conscience. Bell didn't change government policy, but his great intervention against obliteration bombing reignited a debate about the meaning of the idea of a just war in an age when so much of the civilian population was mobilized as part of the war effort. This debate continues to echo in our politics today.

His willingness to argue for a just war in the crucible of war itself, and not in the academic safety of peace-time, distinguishes his action as being of the highest bravery. And his case was not made on the terms of high politics alone, but was also grounded in his experience as a priest. To someone who played such an important part in helping to remarry high culture and Christianity, Bell could not but have felt keenly the destruction of great buildings, irreplaceable libraries and works of art caused by the Allies' blanket bombing.

But the route-march to his fatal decision was also determined in part by his experience of the young airmen stationed nearby, who came to his palace for art classes between their hectic periods of fighting in the air. It was these young men who told him of their moral dilemma in that, while they believed it was their duty to bomb, the carrying out of this order that killed so many civilians made them feel so unworthy that they excluded themselves from receiving the sacrament. Obliteration bombing was therefore for Bell evil for this second reason. It destroyed an individual's moral character, even when that individual was on the side of the victor, just as it damaged the collective moral life of nations.

My spirit rises to Bell, who teaches me that one's apprenticeship may be lifelong. Then, if one is lucky, out of the blue comes an event which requires a response that puts one's life into context. A different ability is acquired by those whose life is set by their moral compass but whose metal remains untested by any dramatic worldly event, and I have little doubt that, had circumstances turned out in this way, Bell would have remained equally true to his life's vocation, knowing that life's aim is to

7

live out one's beliefs truly and fully even if one is not caught up in one of those great classic clashes between Church and state which light up what personal integrity is about.

Conrad Noel

Conrad Noel is not included merely as a useful butt to George Bell, although he certainly serves this purpose. It is true that all the portraits here, with the exception of that of Beveridge, are the result of an invitation to speak, and on this occasion the invitation was to speak in the church that Noel had adorned as its incumbent for more than 30 years. St John the Baptist is a beautiful, cathedral-like building in Thaxted, Essex.

Noel interested me in spite of his Trotskyite political views. Few things could prove less attractive. Noel had much more to his appeal than this idiocy. He was one of the great champions of the Catholic wing of the Church of England that flowered for half a century and added so much beauty to the English liturgy.

It is now difficult to fix clearly what this movement was about. Its successors have largely lost a social application of the gospel that went hand in hand with developing a liturgy so magnificent that for me it evokes more than a hint of the splendour and wonder of God. Indeed, both of these activities were seen as but the different sides of the same coin. 'You cannot claim to worship Jesus in the tabernacle if you do not pity Jesus in the slums.'[6] What was once an extraordinary dual campaign of social action combined with the development of a great and beautiful liturgy has now collapsed into an obsession with church millinery, rather than the militancy to which Noel gave such a cutting edge.

Organizing fights with morris dancers based in neighbouring villages is just one small example of the mischief Noel liked to create. Promoting his insatiable ego was not, however, his main concern, although it was a clear feature throughout his life. But somehow, despite all such distractions, the development of a form of worship through which the wonder of God might be espied remained at the centre of Noel's being.

Eleanor Rathbone

Of all of my heroes, it is Eleanor Rathbone's resolution which I wish I could match in my own life. It is not simply what I perceive as Eleanor's loneliness, and the political isolation of a long-distance political runner, that evinces from me such empathy. Eleanor's appeal goes far beyond this necessary aspect of the professional politician who is committed to causes rather than simply making his or her way up the greasy pole.

Part of Eleanor's appeal certainly comes from a principled life, lived as an outsider being forced to deal with insiders who were mostly time-servers. Yet there is no evidence of her acting in a way that might have opened up the door to that other life for a politician. Churchill, whose ascent to the premiership owes more than a little to Eleanor's efforts, never gave her the opportunity to refuse such an embrace. His consolation prize to her, the offer of a damehood, was elegantly declined.

> The truth is that I have…a distaste for titles…this feeling…is especially strong in war-time, when it is impossible for public honours to be conferred on more than a very few of the millions who are daily risking their lives in dangerous services in which I cannot take part.[7]

Another aspect of Eleanor's attraction for me comes from the way she and William Beveridge forged the robust infant child of the social sciences into an especially effective weapon for political campaigning. She and William were both part of that band of reformers who professionally mastered the benefits that came from social enquiries and moulded them into radical battering rams to force open the doors of privilege. Yet, as well as possessing the moral courage to see these findings through into policy no matter how difficult this might be, Eleanor possessed physical courage in equal measure.

When Eleanor was bombed out of her home in Romney Street, she and her lifelong friend Elizabeth Macadam built a new home literally around the corner in Tufton Street, a home that was also within walking distance of the House of Commons. There they were visited by a young soldier, T. S. Simey, who later became the Charles Booth Professor of Social Science at Liverpool University, which Eleanor's father had played such a key role in founding. As Simey bade Eleanor goodbye for what turned out to be the last time, the two gallant ladies came down to the street from their apartment block to see their young visitor off into the night. Eleanor and Elizabeth seemed oblivious to the bombs that were exploding all around them – this was the same night that, only a block away, Westminster Abbey was hit and, across the road, the House of Commons was set on fire. Yet Simey observed that Eleanor gave no hint of the immediate physical danger that surrounded her, and he took away with him only Eleanor's abiding sense of optimism about the future.

William Beveridge

William Beveridge's success as a reformer is the basis for my admiration for him, and it is a record I wish I could have mirrored so much more accurately in my own life. He was personally awkward, often gauche, shy and certainly arrogant – and, as unattractive as this characteristic is, Beveridge had much to be arrogant about. So, while I believe that Harold Wilson, prime minister and sometime research assistant to Beveridge, probably depicts a side of Beveridge's character that makes the prospect of being locked in a room with him for any length of time a risk too far – he was according to Wilson, 'a bitch' – Beveridge is nevertheless a hero for me. He is quite possibly, through the generosity with which he disposed of his income to his family and other good causes, even a saint.

What Violet Bonham Carter observed about Churchill is equally true of Beveridge. Churchill had commented prior to World War II that a man's life had now to be nailed to the cross of either thought or action. Yet Churchill refused throughout his long life to accept the ruling of the modern world that a person had to plan or perform, conceive or execute. Churchill appeared for so much of his life to have been born out of season. But, as his lifelong friend Lady Violet Bonham Carter realized, the coming of World War II, when every decision was a deed, finally allowed Churchill to enter into his double inheritance.[8]

What was true of Churchill was even more true of Beveridge. Indeed, thought and action characterized practically the whole of his life. For almost half a century Beveridge's life involved constantly gliding between the two worlds of thought and action. There is no one else in our recent history who has bridged this divide with such distinction. It is as if one part of Beveridge's mind focused on the development of research-based policy while the other simultaneously envisaged how such policies might be implemented by their creator.

Beveridge has no peer in either of his two distinct fields of thought and few when it came to action, never mind in their combination. Beveridge crafted his study of unemployment into an academic discipline, and his beliefs about the causes of unemployment formed the basis for the great reforming programme of the 1906 Liberal government. As if not satisfied with this achievement, Beveridge then showed his extraordinary abilities to create the administrative machine that would implement his policies.

Thirty years later Beveridge painted a blueprint of even greater magnitude and his welfare framework is clearly discernible today. Whether it should be is, of course, another matter, but it was only the unlucky spin of the electoral wheel that denied Beveridge the opportunity again to implement the very reforms he had envisaged. As we are now in an age when political parties as we have known them are dying, we may just have the tantalizing prospect of the Beveridge model, with his near-unique qualities of thought and action, coming back into fashion.

These saints and heroes impress me by their clear goodness and disinterestedness, a goodness and disinterestedness that is crucial in public life if society is to prosper and if civilization is to be enhanced. These portraits are offered as an appreciation that we are all part of what the medievalists saw as the great chain of being, so that, perhaps, younger generations will be better able to appreciate that the transmission of values from old to young plays a crucial part in humankind's striving for the good society. This volume is also offered in the hope that, in valuing the contribution that each of these great individuals has made, we may yet be stirred to write a new hymn sheet for our times.

Part 1

THE TEMPLE FAMILY

Introduction

Why do I begin with Frederick Temple and why do I regard
him more highly than his son William? Most people might
argue that William was the 'greater man'. So here I set out the
case for reviewing Frederick's reputation.

Frederick's story excites me. His ascent from a childhood
home headed by a poor and widowed mother to the very apex
of the social order of the British Empire tells us as much about
his character and qualities as about how open Victorian society
was to the very clever. Would the son of a poor single parent
in Britain today, in a country with so many mediocre schools,
have such an opportunity?

It is not, however, only Frederick's ability that excites. His character is equally attractive. He never sold out and never trimmed.
He was never disloyal to those whose friendship perhaps damaged him in the eyes of an Establishment that would decide his
preferment. But consider his record. Frederick's political aim
was nothing less than to revolutionize our country's education.
Meritocracy was to be advanced through a grammar school
network that served the country well for more than a hundred
years until it was smashed by Tony Crosland, aided and abetted
by Mrs T.

William does not quite meet this record. While clearly so
very able, he was nonetheless not sufficiently able to see that
the philosophical framework he spent so much time explaining
and developing was, at the very best, a cul-de-sac. And yet he
was on the side of the angels and is now possibly a member
of that illustrious group. William is also attractive because he
is so much a transitional figure. His father could have stepped
out of the pages of *Boy's Own*. Hero was stamped right through

him. William, his son, steps, by contrast, into the world of celebrity. But William played the part to perfection, and in so doing helped to raise the hopes of working people that our democracy should deliver them a people's peace.

1

Last of the great Victorians[1]

History, as opposed to life, dealt Frederick Temple a rough hand. Temple's request that no biography should be written has meant that, until now, we have observed him mainly through studies of his contemporaries, many of whom were also his rivals. His tenure at Canterbury was short and it came about when he was old and his powers were failing; Temple was not appointed archbishop until he was 75. His stewardship (from 1896 to 1902) occurred at a time when the Victorian age was fast closing, and most bright eyes were determinedly directed at the possibilities opening up with the new century. Frederick has therefore been contrasted unfavourably with his son William – who has been the only person so far to follow in his father's footsteps to the throne of St Augustine. Moreover, while William benefited from the age in which he lived, Frederick lost by living into a period when heroes were giving place to personalities.

Then, to top everything, when – nearly a century later – Peter Hinchliff came along to refocus Frederick Temple's public image, this gifted historian and biographer died just before completing the task. That death denies us the judgement of a knowledgeable and sympathetic observer and robs Temple of a forceful and clear exposition of his lasting value. It is possible, however, from *Frederick Temple, Archbishop of Canterbury: A life* to present a basis for the elder Temple's greatness.

It is, above all, a tale fit for a land of heroes. Here the book displays the late Professor Hinchliff's greatest gifts. From the poor home of a widowed mother, Temple rises, on the basis of scholarship and promotion secured by merit, to the social apex of the British Empire, becoming the most senior person in the kingdom apart from the principal members of the Royal Family. This remarkable record was achieved by an equal application of intellect and very hard work, and by Temple's positioning himself, at considerable risk, on the two big issues of the century – education reform and scientific advance – while refusing to trim on essential questions or on matters of friendship.

By any standards, this is an extraordinary story. At first, Temple was taught at home by a mother who herself had largely to acquire the knowledge before passing it on to her children. When he won a place at his local school, he excelled in Latin; he went on to win a first-class degree in mathematics (as well as classics), but he had initially learned that discipline from a mother who only knew for certain that the children had discovered how to solve the problem by checking the answer book, which was carefully locked away from the examinees.

Educational reformer

On the first of the two great questions of the Victorian age, the impact of scientific knowledge, Hinchliff's touch is most secure. Yet that is but part of the story. Only now is education again beginning to take on the role it then played as the engine-force of both personal achievement and social improvement. We are still too close to an age when ideology was seen as the means of propelling society into the future fully to appreciate the pivotal role education played in the Victorian world-view. And it was on this central stage that – as Simon Green has argued,[2] far more forcibly and effectively than does Hinchliff – Temple has to be seen as the greatest of all Victorian educational reformers.

To the Victorian, education was unquestionably the single means of improving both the character and the conduct of individuals, while safely securing the advances of society as a whole. Temple's record can be criticized only on the issue of extending educational opportunities to the working class; yet it is unclear whether he thought the majority of the working class were incapable of benefiting from secondary education, or whether he believed the country could not afford to make such provision other than for those with the most exceptional talent. So, even here, at the weakest point of Temple's record, the jury remains out. Any 12 men and women would take note of Temple's refusal to seek an easy ascent of the greasy pole: instead of accompanying his erstwhile mentor A. C. Tait – himself a future archbishop – to join his staff at Rugby School, Temple remained at Balliol College, Oxford, before heading the first institution for the training of teachers for poor-law schools.

On every other count, Temple's education record remains without serious question or challenge. He argued for a new use of endowments, and it is hard to overestimate the opposition he thereby encountered. Endowments should reward merit, not simply the poor, irrespective of ability. His stance here was of fundamental importance to the emergence of grammar schools catering for middle-class pupils. He drove home this reform programme through his membership of the Taunton Commission, which sat between 1864 and 1868 and which revealed the poor provision of secondary education as well as the uneven distribution and the misuse of education endowments. Likewise, his successful advocacy of the establishment of the Oxford Local Examination Board ensured not only that the university reached out into this newly emerging schools market but that, simultaneously, university reform ran parallel to the reorganization of secondary education.

Temple also played a seminal role in developing public school education. He did so in the manifesto he presented to the Clarendon Commission,[3] while advancing the cause in a practical manner as headmaster of Rugby, where he had succeeded Tait in 1857 and which was then arguably the premier public school in the country. In a similar vein, Temple set the course for non-sectarian state education.

Advocate of reason

If Hinchliff fails to bring out Temple's dominance in the education debate with sufficient force, no such doubt remains over his handling of scientific advance. Again, it is not easy now to appreciate the way the impact of biblical scholarship, first from Germany, and the scientific advances symbolized by Darwinism shook the relative calm of Victorian religious beliefs. Temple was not alone as a churchman in refusing to be ostrich-like. Hinchliff does not claim originality for him. What he does do is illustrate how, in this debate, Temple was one of the bravest advocates of embracing the new knowledge. The events surrounding *Essays and Reviews*, which was published in 1860 and to which he contributed, are well known: Temple refused to back down over his defence of reason, even when his appointment to the bishopric at Exeter was brought into question, nine years later. (The next essay discusses how *Essays and Reviews* ricocheted back on to Frederick's career.)

But Frederick's stance did not prevent his promotion to the bishopric of London and then finally, if all too briefly, to the peak as Archbishop of Canterbury. Temple's descent into death began, appropriately enough, as he advocated in the House of Lords the measure which became Balfour's 1902 Education Act. But that was not before he had crowned Edward VII king. Nearly blind, Temple was the first to pay homage. The old man, frail and unstable, was unable to stand after kneeling at the feet of his monarch. Peter Hinchliff records one report of the King raising Temple to his feet. In gratitude, the old Primate touched the King's crown and offered a blessing. The King immediately caught hold of the old man's hand and kissed it.

2

Father and son:
the relative abilities of
Frederick and William Temple

It is likely that William Temple always felt inferior to his father, Frederick. This intriguing insight into William Temple's character was offered by Stephen Spencer, who himself has written on William's prophetic role.[1]

There can be no doubting the quality of Frederick. Raised and initially taught by his widowed mother and surviving on his scholarship at Balliol, Frederick was so poor that during the winter nights he worked on the staircase, using the public light to read. Yet, as we have seen, from these most humble beginnings Frederick rose by his own efforts to the highest social position in the land outside the immediate Royal Family.

A taker of risks

Frederick's life was built on taking risks. He rejected the offer of his patron, A. C. Tait, to go to Rugby as a master. Instead of opting for the high road to advancement, Frederick chose instead to head a college training teachers for poor-law schools – a college in its infancy, at that. He did later go to Rugby, but this time as headmaster. Just before his appointment there Frederick contributed to *Essays and Reviews*, a collection of essays by different contributors attempting to embrace the new biblical learning within a Christian cosmology.[2] Here was his first taste of the kind of opposition which the book met.

This contribution on education gives an insight into the quality of Frederick's character. Contributing to *Essays and Reviews* was more than a high-risk strategy. Its publication was viewed as a full-frontal attack on Christian orthodoxy, as the work attempted to take into some account the advances that had been made over the previous decades in biblical scholarship, particularly the work originating in Germany. While this initiative passed off in terms of changing a key debate in Victorian England, more immediately, in the ecclesiastical politics of the time, it marked Frederick out as at best someone not possessing a safe pair of hands and at worst a person of unorthodox, if not heterodox, thinking.

Frederick took few prisoners in the fall-out which resulted from such risk-taking. When, at the outset of the controversy, Tait, by then Bishop of London, supported the Archbishop of Canterbury's condemnation of *Essays and Reviews*, Frederick expressed his dismay at what he clearly regarded as an act of near treachery by his mentor. He knew Tait's views too well to believe that this was anything but a piece of political posturing by his one-time champion. One can only wonder whether Frederick ever fully trusted Tait again.

The opposition to *Essays and Reviews* did not die. The book continued to enrage sections of the Church so much that, almost a decade later, a public campaign was run to prevent Frederick's appointment as Bishop of Exeter. Then, as now, the Crown's nominee for a bishopric has to be approved by a cathedral chapter. A chapter rejecting the Crown's candidate is liable to all the penalties of *praemunire* – loss of all civil rights, with the forfeiture of lands, goods and chattels, and imprisonment during the royal pleasure. Even so, seven of the 20 chapter members voted against Temple's nomination – possibly the most controversial appointment ever in terms of votes. Friends sought to persuade Temple that he should withdraw his essay

22

from the volume and so ease his promotion to the bench of bishops. Instead, Frederick stood by his work, and that of his fellow contributors, until his enthronement at Exeter. The cathedral chapter had to elect him, and he had to be enthroned, before any public move was made. And even then Frederick's agreement to withdraw his section from future editions only became known when a colleague publicly disclosed the private conversation he had had with Frederick on his views and intentions about the volume.[3]

A lesser being?

With such talents and rugged individuality, it would not be surprising if William did not feel a lesser being than his father, for which son of a successful father does not? Moreover, William was born when Frederick was a month short of his sixtieth birthday. His was not a childhood advancing to manhood in the shadow of a father making his way in the world. His father had already made his name when William was born. No surprise, then, that William was in awe of his father. It was as though courage ran through Frederick's very veins.

Remember the length of isolation Frederick was prepared to endure to defend the approach and the contributions to *Essays and Reviews*. Compare that confrontation of bigotry with his son's behaviour when confronting an equally objectionable piece of prejudice, this time against women. Journeying to Cuddesdon, an Anglo-Catholic training college for priests, to attend an executive meeting of the Life and Liberty campaign (ironically, the campaign to win independence for the Church of England), he was informed that Maude Royden would not be allowed to stay the night in this all-male theological college. Royden was one of the more advanced radicals on William Temple's campaign and was a pioneer in persuading the Church to re-evaluate the role of women's ministry, becoming finally an advocate of women priests a decade before practically any other public figure. Instead of moving the meeting to a more hospitable environment, William allowed Royden to resign and to travel back to London alone. There is no doubting William's radicalism, but it was a radicalism which operated within severely defined limits. William was a very accomplished ecclesiastical water-spider, skimming across the political waters without leaving much impression behind him.[4] (It is an analogy which also fits many of Tony Blair's activities.)

There was more than meets the eye to Frederick's rough exterior and the ease with which William moved among the Establishment. The determined West Country accent of the father, and the easy flowing upper-class accent of the son symbolized a fundamental difference in approach. Was maintaining that accent the outward visible sign that Frederick had not been captured by the Establishment? Or, if it was, was any capturing done on his own terms? Frederick's words and actions were as straight as a die. No concessions were made to offering up the right soundbite, or of being concerned one iota about how his actions might be viewed. Any hint at pretence or dissembling would lead Temple senior to end the conversation and his support, as Ben Tillett, one of the dockers' leaders, found in double-quick time during the famous 1889 dock strike.

Conversely, it was not William's style to be confrontational. During the General Strike, Prime Minister Baldwin, provoked by church leaders' public action which damaged the private negotiations seeking a settlement, asserted that the churches had no more business to try to settle the coal dispute than the Federation of British Industry had in seeking to revise the Athanasian Creed.[5] There can be little doubt that, had Frederick ever got himself into such a position, his response would have come in equal measure, rising to the FBI's redrafting challenge. There is no recorded reply from William to this prime minister-ial rebuff, although, as we shall see later, the Prime Minister's gibe had hit home (see p. 32).

On another front, too, William comes out 'less than equal' to his father. Frederick was one of life's natural conservatives, and one who was naturally sympathetic to injustices to individuals and classes. It never occurred to him that the settled order could be changed to any radical degree, and so it was within such a framework that Frederick expressed his sympathy. But once he decided upon a course there was little others could do to dissuade him. When Frederick hit upon the idea that the poor of Lambeth should have a park he moved to give half his garden at Lambeth to form a public park for them. Lambeth Palace then possessed one of the largest private gardens in London. Davidson, who as Bishop of Winchester was waiting in the wings to inherit Frederick's post with the palace garden intact, set out secretly to frustrate the Primate's plan.

Frederick had been in the habit of actively seeking the views and advice of Davidson, whom he probably saw as his successor. On being exposed, Davidson wrote sycophantically to Frederick, expressing the hope that his behind-the-scenes action should not lead to his banishment from the position of the Primate's trusted advisor. Frederick replied that Davidson's less than straightforward behaviour would go unpunished, but that, under his freehold rights, half of Lambeth's garden would nonetheless go to form a public park.[6] And so it remains to this day.[7]

In stark contrast, William went in for 'isms'. By 1908 he was proclaiming his socialism, and that the choice facing a poor, confused electorate was quite simply socialism or heresy. In adopting this stance, William, I believe, mistook the rhetoric for what was the underlying significance. Christian Socialism, as it became known, had little to do with socialism and everything to do with expressing sympathy with the downtrodden while seeking immediate ways to relieve their oppression.

This movement reached its height with the Christian Social Union (CSU), by far and away the most effective and impressive of church radical groups. It is easy to ridicule any such group.

Edward Norman pokes fun at their silliness, their pomposity and, more importantly, their blindness to their class view of the world. But to say, as he does, that the CSU was 'central, respectable and vague' is to miss the point.[8] This is precisely where the group wished to be and where they thought they would be most politically effective. Given how ruthlessly the class card was played against the Labour interest, well beyond the period of the CSU, gaining political respectability is the first and most crucial status any radical movement must achieve in Britain. Vagueness is itself a somewhat imprecise term, yet it did not rule out some very effective campaigns. The secondary picketing of shops selling goods made with sweated labour is a tactic that the most militant of today's left-wing groups have spurned, perhaps on grounds that such campaigns take a great deal of organizing and involve sustained hard work. It was within this 'vague' radical tradition, and not the expression of socialist enthusiasm, that William was to make such an effective contribution to the development of radical politics.

Two outstanding public servants

Which of these two extraordinary characters – father or son – wielded the greater influence? Both made judgements about the role of the established Church in English politics. In a single blast, by recording that Anglican worshippers no longer composed the majority of Sunday attendees, the 1851 census had holed the Anglican dominance of religious life in Great Britain, and holed it below the waterline. But, unlike the case of the *Titanic*, the hierarchy refused to let the symbolism attached to a national Church sink. That was essentially Frederick's position. However, as William became active on the national stage after World War I, what he saw was markedly different from what his father had seen only twenty years before.

Frederick's life had been lived during one of the most extraordinary times in England. The country was religious to a degree that many Muslim countries are today, although that mid-century census showed that times were already changing. As the nation began its slow withdrawal from Christianity, many Victorians convinced themselves that people in cities failed to go to church simply because of the lack of a local place of worship. This belief led to one of the most extraordinary church-building programmes ever devised.

Against a policy that saw recovery in terms of outward structures, such as building churches, Frederick developed a political strategy that became his life's work. And it is at this point that one of the sharpest contrasts emerges between these two outstanding public servants. Frederick was an outsider who superbly played the hand of an insider. William, who was an insider, adopted a strategy of one of nature's outsiders.

It needs to be said that Frederick's activities were planned during the high point of Victorian confidence and that such a role could be expected from someone who was clearly destined for the top. But this should not detract from the way Frederick deployed his considerable talents to the greatest effect. William's public life, in comparison, was lived out after the First World War shattered the Victorian dream of a self-governing nation, all singing, so to speak, from the same hymn sheet. A comment has already been made in the first essay about how, through sheer effort and ability, Frederick stakes a claim to be the greatest of Victorian education reformers and that he achieved this by becoming a consummately successful insider. Frederick's stance was that successful social change could only come about by changing individuals and that, to achieve this, education was the most powerful of tools with which to mould a new society. He used his position on the great official reforming commissions of Victorian England to promote the idea of a meritocracy. He linked his proposed secondary education changes to university reform, so that the universities reached out into an expanding schools market. And between commissions he pursued his objective through essays, sermons, journal articles and, last but not least, his position in the legislature that came once he was consecrated Bishop of Exeter.

Simon Green sees Frederick as having a claim to be the 'greatest of all Victorian education reformers' and, because education was seen then (as it is once again becoming to be seen) as the most powerful of all agents for change, to be one of Victorian England's great social reformers. His originality Green sees as deriving not from espousing new dogma, but from the way he combined a number of ideas and structured his campaign so that other people recognized a new relationship between each of them. Green observes that Macaulay was an early advocate of meritocracy, Coleridge was more famous for advocating a role for the clerisy (i.e. made up of literary or educated people, rather than just the clergy) and Arnold was a finer exponent of liberal culture; but no one combined these three key concepts into such an effective political ideology as did Frederick.[9]

William was less sanguine about the political effectiveness of an established Church, as well he might be, as priests reported their experiences caring for the soldiers who faced imminent death at the front line.[10] Despite being members of an established Church, few of the privates in the trenches had much idea of what Christianity was about, although large sums of church treasure had been spent on what had been believed to be the churching of the nation. William immediately saw how fundamental a challenge this constituted and how his political life would be very different from the one lived by his father. Frederick worked at the apex where the Church, the court, Parliament and Whitehall merged. William occupied the very same position, but power, as so often, was moving on. Hence the *raison d'être* of his life was to try to reassert Christianity at the centre of the nation's life, and in order to do this he had to change the way the nation perceived the Anglican Church.[11]

Frederick took it for granted that he would wield power in the state. William realized, as the political ground was shifting, that for a bishop or an archbishop merely to say something no longer carried the absolute weight it once did. If Frederick's political influence was lived out on dry land, William was not only at sea but was also forced to test the effectiveness of the map and compass inherited from a once all-powerful established Church.

William's map and compass were his belief in God and in the role of reason and tradition. That William never doubted the existence of God has to be appreciated. It governed his every action. Moreover, William's life was about communicating his central belief in the truth of Christianity. It was a truth which could not be confined to the private activities of individuals. Its rule was as relevant to the thinking of public figures, and their actions, as it was accepted in the confessional.

A large part of William's appeal in the country, and therefore a crucial part of his political power, was the means by which he was able to convey in every public action this central belief in God, and in a God who was of this world as well as of the next. If anything, this belief became stronger as the years passed. What did change was the means by which William sought to convey this belief and what flowed from it. The following essays look at the steady development of his political strategy, from a campaign to reform the Church of England's position vis-à-vis the state, as a means of influencing the latter, to one of establishing powerful church pressure groups which could advance his socio-political objectives to both Church and nation and, last, the means by which he sought to address the nation directly.

Repositioning the Church

By the time William had come of age ecclesiastically, the threat to the established Church's position came not from disestablishment campaigns – the great alliance of nonconformity and Liberalism was over – but from the increased secularization of life which made the established Church seem at best old-fashioned and at worst irrelevant. How could the Anglican Church become once again relevant and therefore politically powerful?

This was the central question to which William addressed himself. His answer, at first, was the Life and Liberty movement which, as we have seen, aimed to free the Church of state interference.[12] William spearheaded this campaign, and so that he could devote himself full-time to its work he resigned his plum living at St James's, Piccadilly.

Temple made the most of the advantage accruing to the son of an archbishop, unmercifully lobbying his father's successor at Canterbury, Randall Davidson. Whereas Davidson and most of the hierarchy wished for modest reform, so that they could go on governing the Church of England in the time-accustomed manner with their position strengthened, the radical elements of Life and Liberty wanted disestablishment, which would have meant disendowment. Hence the bishops' opposition to any idea that might involve the loss of the Church's historic assets. The campaign resulted in the 1919 Enabling Act.

William cannily saw that an establishment position offered opportunities of playing a major political role in British society. That political advantage was not to be unthinkingly surrendered. To others in the Life and Liberty campaign, disestablishment was an ideological objective. Not so with William, who was ever pragmatic in his political approach. A compromise was struck: the Church Assembly was born.

However, it soon became very obvious to William that the Assembly was not going to be the body which would reposition the Church in the eyes of the masses. As a political animal, William was forever considering which vehicle offered him the greatest means of wielding influence.

The first such body went under the unprepossessing name of the Conference on Christian Politics, Economics and Citizenship (Copec), held in Birmingham in 1924, which is explored in greater detail on p. 53.[13] While Temple was clearly the 'mind and muscle' of the Life and Liberty campaign, in Copec he shared that burden with Joe Oldham, a veteran ecumenical leader and Christian social ethicist, and still a much under-valued figure in the development of the kind of social philosophy which William so favoured (see Chapter 5 for more details).

While Archbishop Davidson, who had succeeded William's father to the top post, was able to resist the blandishments of Mr and Mrs William Temple to come to stay with them (William had married Frances Anson in 1916), he found no effective way of preventing the delivery of William's missives through the post. Temple's approach was clear. It had been set out in a letter to Randall Davidson as part of the bombardment strategy of the Life and Liberty campaign. Temple wrote to his archbishop that, in his view, the Church 'is commissioned to bring to bear upon all phases and problems of life, political, social, economic, no less than personal, the mind of Christ wherein alone is to be found the true basis of human life'.

It is not hard to appreciate the shock such a declaration must have had on poor old Davidson's system and sense of ecclesias-tical decorum. Here in Copec was a much more determined challenge to the status quo of privatized religion. Yet Copec did not provide the political breakthrough for which Temple hoped. He met with some success in influencing the debate within the Church, but William never fooled himself that church gather-ings by themselves led to political influence, let alone power. William's main objective was for a Church which could influence national political developments in the direction of the social Christianity about which he believed so passionately.

Commenting on the Church's involvement in politics, William remarked that when individuals demanded that the Church should do something they usually meant that the bishop should say something. Saying something was only important to Temple if it could lead to action. But Temple found himself increasingly saying rather than doing things. This failure can be measured by the way Temple moved from group to group, as if it was a failure of organization which led to William's lack of influence.

The war-time Malvern Conference aimed at picking up the debate where Copec left off. Driven out of London by the war-time bombing, delegates invited themselves and assembled to plan a Christian response to the likely shape of the post-war world. Temple was anxious that after the war the Church should play a politically more effective role than it had achieved in 1918. While delegates were no doubt suitably uplifted from meeting in freezing halls during 1941, the main beneficiary, as from all of these activities, was Temple himself. He used these gatherings, perhaps subconsciously, as a modern politician uses a think tank. Within these organizations ideas were debated and, from their membership, support groups for Temple were established. It was from these deliberations at Malvern that Temple was able to launch his only really effective political move.[14] Malvern helped sharpen the argument and give greater political direction to his next major political effort.

Christianity and Social Order

The writing of *Christianity and Social Order* was completed quickly and followed the lines William wanted to emerge from the 1941 Malvern Conference. The book nevertheless has a surprisingly defensive tone to it. Almost half of its pages are taken up in arguing the Church's right to 'interfere' in politics – William's choice of word. For someone who was essentially arguing a medieval cosmology to explain the Church's right to be active in public life it is a surprising and unwarranted concession. Surely the Church could behave in no other way? J. M. Keynes, to whom William sent a draft, made such a point. William, after all, always argued that the world operated on God's patch. Baldwin's quip all those years ago during the General Strike had clearly hit home (see p. 24).

It is only towards the middle of the book that the serious argument begins, with the most concise summary of Christian doctrine. In 11 pages William manages to summarize all the main arguments about God and his purpose, together with the dignity, tragedy and destiny of humankind.

The main line of this little volume, as in all William's socio-political works, stresses the fundamental importance of society being organized so as to ensure that each individual could fulfil his or her potential. In William's hands, this was to become a two-edged argument. The state had a duty to arrange its affairs so that each individual would be able to develop his or her talents to the full. But none of us would be fully free or fully developed unless we had the right relationship with God.

This central plea for so organizing society put William's appeal into what I see as the richest radical tradition in modern England. English Idealism, in the view of Henry Scott Holland, the founder of the CSU among much else, had done a great deal to bolster the Christian belief of many radicals who might otherwise, at the turn of the nineteenth century, have opted purely for a materialistic philosophy. T. H. Green, the high priest of English Idealism, in Scott Holland's words had given 'us back the language of self-sacrifice and taught how we belonged to one another in the one life of organic humanity. He filled us again with the breath of high idealism.'[15]

Yet this set of ideas was not one meant for professional scholars and philosophers alone. Its aim was to produce a particular type of public servant, of which William was himself a prime example. Here was Green's greatest strength, in that his ideas permeated the atmosphere in which public life was conducted. These public servants were not simply on hand to carry out the radical reform programme of their political masters, but themselves helped to build a political culture in which politics was seen as a collective endeavour to advance the interests of the whole community.

The incoming tide of doubt was swelled for many by the impact of biblical scholarship, which as we have noted Frederick had done his best to turn to the advantage of faith, and the gains in the natural sciences, again a topic on which Frederick was anxious to make part of the Christian cosmology. Against this tide, Green offered an alternative presentation of the great truths which could be defended rationally. And he attracted other followers who could not accept Christian dogma but wished to maintain Christian morality. Idealism certainly provided William with an alternative, and I cannot help thinking that its appeal, as described by Scott Holland, proved to be a more attractive framework for William's radical politics than did his Christian faith alone. In particular, by centring political activity on the full development of each individual's personality and awarding education the primary means of achieving this objective, William drew on the power of the English Idealist tradition to project the relevance of his Christian vision. In other words, William, consciously or not, was attempting 'to do a T. H. Green in reverse', by putting a Christian belief back at the heart of the Idealist ideology.

Christianity and Social Order's strength was not confined to its pitch into the centre of English radical belief. There could have been no more propitious time for *Christianity and Social Order*'s entry on to the national stage. Allied victories in the Western Desert signalled that, although the war was far from won, the Allies would eventually win. With this victory, the mind of voters turned to a new world to replace the 'decade of deceit', as Auden termed the 1930s from the safety of the USA, to where he had retreated. Into this world *Christianity and Social Order* was delivered, as was, incidentally, the Beveridge Report (of which more in Chapter 12). Both sold in record numbers to an eager public wanting a message of hope and a belief that a new world was possible.

It was also at this time that a Gallup poll showed a swing to the left which was to deliver Labour an historic election victory three years later.[16] In this leftward move, an appeal for a better yesterday, in the words of Peter Hennessy, played a not insignificant role.[17] *Christianity and Social Order*, with its ideas so rooted in Edwardian England, conveyed a warmth and security which people rightly or wrongly associated with that age and which they desperately wanted to revisit. Those ideas may have failed to deliver a land fit for heroes in 1918, but they could be used this time to carve out a better tomorrow, and that they certainly did.

Although this was a volume which conjured up a quintessential appeal to English decencies, it was one which also incorporated the 'middle ground' language of the 1930s. Central planning and the much enhanced role of the state were promoted at the expense of non-state forms of collective provision. Here William was part block-builder of the post-1945 consensus, and while that consensus is now not only being questioned but replaced, it was then probably an inevitable stage through which British radicalism would travel.

In *Christianity and Social Order*, coming as it did at the end of a 20-year career as a bishop and archbishop, William helped raise people's hopes and legitimate expectations. William was as important as anyone in convincing the electorate both that it was safe to vote for radical change and that radical change was what the poor and the working class should demand. To the middle class he sold the idea of a continuing sacrifice, while for the working class and the poor he helped to convince them that their position of deference in British politics was coming to a close. Although William died in September 1944, his lasting influence was to be seen almost a year later as the ballot papers were strewn across the counting tables. Clement Attlee emerged with a record parliamentary majority, in no small measure thanks to the life of political campaigning by Frederick Temple's son William.

3

William Temple's business ethics: stymieing the left for a generation

William Temple was much more than a conventional product of the privileged Victorian upper-middle class into which he was born. He was part of the Christian Socialist tradition that saw itself as the first group of Christians since the collapse of the medieval hegemony to make a sustained criticism of the economic order. In fact, as the literature of the Victorian period shows only too well, such criticism was fierce, with churchmen at the centre of this debate. While William had an immediate and beneficial impact on the politics that prepared the ground for a radical Labour government, his record is rather different when it comes specifically to his economic ideas. His views on this aspect of our daily life helped reap a bitter harvest during the 1970s and 1980s when Labour was most vulnerable and prey to disingenuous political and economic doctrines.

An early radical

We do not know the source of William's amazingly strong social conscience. On practically all of the interesting aspects of the future primate's personal life his biographer remains curiously silent.[1] All we are left with is a tantalizing scrap of information about young William on holiday with his parents. In appreciating its significance, we need to remember the changed economic position of chicken and beef. Unlike today, in the 1890s chicken was something of a luxury, while beef was a common dish.

As the assembled family began tucking into the luckless bird William burst into tears. How unfair, he bemoaned, that the servants were being denied the joy he was about to savour. Beef was their lot. From this point onwards, William set his eyes on a radical path which would make his life as different as it could have been from his father's – although both of them landed safely in the seat of St Augustine at the end of their distinguished careers.

William's father was, without any question, sympathetic to the needs of the poor and, more generally, to working-class interests. How else could he be, given his own humble background and his burning sense of integrity? But although Frederick's life extended just beyond the start of the new century, he was in every sense a nineteenth-century figure. He would have hated today's emphasis on soundbites and the reign of spin doctors, laundering every thought and action of public figures. Any hint of pretence, actual or imagined, would lead Temple senior to end the conversation. Sizing up friend and foe alike was just one of Frederick's uncanny gifts. It was not one which was passed on in the genes. Michael Ramsey, no sloth when it comes to praising William Temple, commented on his predecessors' judgement of character: 'Cosmo was flawless, Temple was hopeless, Fisher was superb; I am erratic.'[2] Part of the attraction of William was his enduring boyish naivety. Another was enthusiasm.

Oxford Idealism

The Balliol to which William went was markedly different from the college his father had attended all those decades before. Many of the undergraduates of William's years fell under the spell of T. H. Green. Against what had become an incoming tide of doubt – swelled for so many by the impact of biblical scholarship, which William's father had done his best to incorporate into faith, and the advance of the natural sciences, again a topic which Frederick was anxious to make part of Christian

37

thinking – Green offered a haven of safety for those, among others, whose religious beliefs might otherwise have cracked. Green's philosophy certainly allowed those wishing to do good to explain the rationale for their actions in terms which had been familiar for centuries.

Green was not the only person to make a lasting impression on young William. Idealism was absorbed into Labour politics and became part of a Christian Socialist appeal. William grew to manhood during the second wave of Christian Socialist ideas, perhaps more correctly spoken of as Christian Socialist Idealism. The first efforts – the founding of Christian Socialism – had collapsed, ironically under the unbending will of its founder, F. D. Maurice. To Maurice we owe a special debt for freeing us from any fear of a literal eternity in hell-fire. He was also an advocate, perhaps unsurprisingly, of limited liability in economic life. Yet this gentlest and most courageous of men could sometimes appear as bigoted as those whom he opposed. It was he who ruthlessly disbanded the attempts of his followers to build upon the early beginnings of Christian Socialism.

We have to wait until the Guild of St Matthew and, more importantly, the Christian Social Union (CSU) before the second spring opens before our eyes. As we have seen, Edward Norman pokes fun at their silliness, their pomposity, their blindness to their class view of the world and their vagueness.[3] But their vagueness and upper-class membership did nothing to frighten the electorate. We are, it is important to remember, recalling a period when an appeal had to be made to that minority of the population who had the vote. In this gentle, very English way, the CSU played an important role in changing public opinion about the justice of the poor's cause, and thereby helped to determine the path radical politics took in this country. CSU strategy did not result, as the members wished, in the conversion of the working classes into practising church-going Christians. But its impact on the development of radical politics should not be ignored.

Law of radical politics

It is a law of radical politics in Britain, and perhaps elsewhere, that radicals rewrite history. The past age was full to overflowing with blemishes. Little was right. Order had collapsed. Unfairness reigned. Reform is long overdue and becomes the demand of the day.

We have all heard this refrain. If I restrict myself to the safety of church politics we can see this aspect of the British radicalism flourishing. Take the Tractarians as an example. They pictured the Church in the eighteenth century as never having sunk so low. Faith was offered on the *à la carte* principle. Bishops rarely resided in their dioceses, rectors and vicars were all too often absent from their parishes, pluralism reigned. The congregations, should they bother to turn up on a Sunday, threw their hats and coats on the altar table, and this was only if the church was not falling into disrepair. Hence the rationale for the revolution or, as they would claim, the counter-revolution that Tractarianism aimed to bring about. It was not until the 1930s, and with the work of Norman Sykes, that the Tractarian line was shown to contain more than a generous portion of propaganda.[4]

The Christian Socialists were no exceptions to this radical law. The cry was disarmingly simple. The Church had never taken seriously the plight of the poor or the justifiable claims of the working class. This performance had to be changed. Christian Socialism was to achieve precisely this. The claim was, of course, absurd. Their charge was repeated with such ferocity but rarely questioned.

It is here that Edward Norman's book is so valuable. In it we find important figures in the hierarchy opposed to the advent and then the spread of the factory system. Once established, a main driving force for many inner-city clergy was the relief of the appalling poverty they witnessed in their parishes. Forgotten are the hundred-and-one ways in which devoted parish priests attended to the needs and comforts of their poorer parishioners – the day school, the orphanage, the infant nursery, youth clubs, breakfasts for the destitute, soup kitchens, clothing clubs, mutual benefit clubs, sick dispensaries: the list is almost endless. Here was a welfare state organized at a parish level. By today's standards and national income, we would find it wanting. When judged by the aspirations and expectations of the time, a very different balance sheet emerges. Likewise, almost no mention was made on this chargesheet of the Church's mainstay role in education, which was also organized at a parish level.

It would be equally wrong to claim that everything possible was accomplished. Nor was the record uniform. Given human nature, there must have been idle, feckless priests, just as there are today. But the record boards of incumbents inside so many churches tell their own story: of priests who stayed in one parish for practically the whole of their working lives, seeing their role of parish priest as the highest of callings, and whose life, work and example helped sanctify the lives of many of their parishioners living in those collections of hovels which made up all too many a parish in nineteenth-century industrial England.

Christian Socialist history

Christian Socialists were wrong in respect of another of their main charges. In their blanket criticism of all events past, and particularly the allegation that the Church had not, since the Reformation at least, attempted to lay down the principles within which the economy operated, the Christian Socialists could not have been more wrong. The charge sheet should have been more narrowly drawn. What the group really objected to was the support Christians gave to the then current laissez-faire orthodoxy. Yet in doing so they saw in their own approach no danger that a future generation would judge their actions in just the same way as they railed against their forebears. It was the young turks of the hierarchy, after all, who, in the 1820s and 1830s were a driving force for establishing the new political economy, and with it a reform of the old Poor Laws. The reform was not sold, of course, on the grounds of grinding the faces of the poor, but on those of tackling poverty. Then, as so often afterwards, the views of the reforms in the hierarchy were unrepresentative of most rank-and-file clergy. The 1834 Poor Law was in fact opposed by many of the parish clergy, who hankered after an age of settled obligations and duties.

The Anglican hierarchy, as Edward Norman has observed, has regularly been taken prisoner by a newly emerging political orthodoxy. Few of the campaigners seemed to realize that the hierarchy had quite a track record in establishing the new political economy against which the Christian Socialists protested. The sheer extent of this influence is apparent from the reply Temple received when he sent *Christianity and Social Order* in manuscript form to J. M. Keynes, asking for his comments on the section defending the Church's right to 'interfere' in temporal matters. Keynes replied: 'along with one line of origin at least, economics more properly called political economy is a side of ethics'. Keynes went on to write that during the eighteenth century, leaving aside the Scots and foreign residents in London, 'I can think of no-one of importance in the development of politico-economic ideas, apart from Bentham, who was not a clergyman, and in most cases a high dignitary in the Church.' Keynes then rattled off the names of Swift, Fleetwood, Paley, Sumner and Malthus.[5]

Indeed, what Norman says of F. D. Maurice and Bishop Westcott – president of the CSU – surely applies more generally to theological thinking then and now. These two individuals

> had a tremendous impact on modern theological learning and there are soundly based reasons why this has been so. They adjusted the relationship between the sacred and the secular in order to see the world as a single unity in the providential design of God.[6]

Perhaps without realizing, this quotation grounds Norman's own criticisms of so much of church radical politics. Ideas cannot be simply and brutally compartmentalized into the sacred (theological) and the profane (political economy) as Norman so often seems to suggest in his work. Once you accept, as Norman appears to do, that the providential order is apparent in everyday life and not merely confined to scriptural texts, then it is more reasonable to start from the world – as William did – and move the argument towards God, than it is to begin the other way around. Of course, the first approach is more open to being captured by the latest political 'faddism'. But the other method is equally open to being taken prisoner by a theological stance that is the product of a bygone age.

Credit, profits and competition

So let us put aside the arcane argument as to whether or not Temple's theology merely peddled the latest fashionable left-wing objective. A much more important task is to examine Temple's economic philosophy and its impact on the politics of the left. Temple was concerned with three issues: credit, profits and competition.

That Temple knew virtually nothing about economic theory was probably an advantage. Much more serious was his total ignorance of the actual workings of the economy. That, of course, does not make him unique. The sad fact is that most of Britain's governing establishment still know precious little. There is, however, no evidence that Temple expended more than a slight effort to acquire any detailed knowledge of finance and banking upon which he so clearly relished pronouncing. Here is the side-effect, if ever there was one, of that Oxbridge education boosting confidence at the expense of any knowledge of the real world. The only work in this field which he is known to have read was that by Sir Ronald Rowe, the title of whose tract, *The Root of All Evil*, tells us practically everything about his objectivity.[7]

There are no surprises about the analyses or the panaceas offered by Rowe to the unsuspecting reader, although the description of 'our behaviour' has a contemporary ring. Here we are told about how the money supply is continually varied 'solely by the action of the banks' and of the fact that the public has 'to an astonishing extent' remained ignorant of what is going on. The inevitable outcome was 'a great gap between rich and poor'. Through its central control of money the small ultra-rich class was gaining ever greater power over the rest of us. This had 'been the root of all our present troubles' at both a national and an international level.

Do I need to continue? The line is obvious. It was, sadly, one Temple gulped down, like the most willing of disciples. It was an 'analysis' of this kind which led him and numerous others into a long flirtation with the idea of social credit. This great economic panacea peddled by progressive opinion in the interwar years was spearheaded by the Archbishop's allies in the Christendom Group. Social credit, as 'the new royal remedy' was called,[8] was the brainchild of Major C. H. Douglas, a distinguished civil engineer, and A. R. Orange, who gave up promoting the idea of re-establishing a medieval system of national guilds to become the new high priest of the movement.

Social credit's basic idea was that society was under the thumb of the bankers, who had seized the power of the creation of credit and were using this power to their own selfish ends. Solution: take over this power and create credit to be used for the public good. In an instant, every dream could be transformed into reality.

More interesting, however, was the movement's view on underconsumption, which was relevant to the economic conditions of the 1930s. But this crucial insight was lost in a bogus analysis. The income generated by industry in the form of wages, salaries and dividends was inadequate, it was alleged, to buy the goods and services produced. Douglas even estimated that this shortage sometimes reached a staggering 90 per cent.

The social credit lobby's appeal to Temple was that the banking system was again put in the dock and stood accountable for most current ills. Yet, as Geoffrey Crowther observed, everyone should have been put on their guard by the social credit campaigners' guarantee of 'the abolition of poverty, the reduction of the likelihood of war to zero, rapidly diminishing crime, the beginning of economic freedom for the individual and the introduction of the leisure state – and all by means of simple book-keeping'.[9]

With claims like that, social credit needed no political health warning. The electorate was quick to make up its own mind. Much more serious, however, were Temple's views on competition and the profit motive – the two mainsprings of a market economy. Here, unfortunately, his legacy was much more enduring.

The Archbishop would have us believe that the basis for his economic ideas was a grounding in the Fathers and in a series of church reports on the operation of the economy. There is little evidence in his work to support this assertion. Much more important were the ideas of R. H. Tawney, one of Temple's closest friends, and those official reports for which Tawney was, to all practical purposes, the author.

Tawney's influence

As Temple arrived at Rugby Station to begin his first term at Rugby School, he met Richard Harry Tawney on the platform. They immediately became friends and remained so for life. Radicals understandably still feel a sense of enchantment when thinking about Tawney. He was in every sense a bridge from public life into academia, one which now, sadly, rarely exists. Those splendid phrases show all the signs of a writer brought up on not only the King James Bible and Cranmer's graceful collects, but also the glorious prose of John Bunyan. If the rhythm of Tawney's prose owes much to the first two sources, much of the imagery comes from Bunyan.

The Victorian intellectual aristocracy, depicted by Noel Annan, lived on.[10] Tawney married William Beveridge's sister. Janet, given Tawney's total detachment from immediate material affairs, was perhaps understandably concerned about money. The emptying of used tea leaves into the stock pot, or the placing of mutton chops for Tawney's and Temple's supper behind a line of books in Tawney's study, was perhaps a pattern of behaviour understandable for someone living with a saint.

Tawney's history was highly political – but no more than most. He told the tale of a medieval Church's concern for ordering economic activity around a just price system, of the system being eroded and then overthrown by the Reformers. The message had wide appeal. Even reactionaries such as Dean Inge of St Paul's could be moved to condemn without any reservation the 'vulgarity of industrial competition'.

More importantly, from the turn of the century Christian Socialists were gathering in a rich harvest from official church reports. *The Moral Witness of the Church on Economic Subjects* was approved by the Canterbury Convocation in 1907 and depicted what were fast becoming, in church circles, the familiar objections to the competitive basis of industrial organization. Only a year later, a Lambeth Conference report on *The Moral Witness of the Church* felt so secure about the evils of competition that it flung reason aside in its attack on the democratic process itself: the democratic ideal had a limited vision and appealed 'too much to individual selfishness or the class interest'.[11]

The climax of this whole movement was to be seen in the reports of the commissions established by the archbishops in 1916. That five commissions planning for the future were established during a war which gave every appearance then of being unending says something about the upper-class confidence of Charles Gore (the Bishop of Oxford), but probably owes more to Archbishop Davidson's sagacity in knowing when to give ground.

The fifth report, *Christianity and Industrial Problems*, is billed as the 'outstanding' expression of Christian thought about post-war society.[12] It was certainly a total triumph for Tawney's line. He was, of course, a member of the commission. The report emphasized the 'lamentable' failure of the Church's recent witness, its absorption in ambulance-type activities in preference to attacking the system and its ideology, which wrought such havoc on the lives of ordinary people. While Christian Social ethics of the New Testament take only two of the 147 pages of the report, the role of the medieval Church gains, perhaps not surprisingly, over nine times that space. A review of recent developments in Christian Social ethics was accomplished in a mere two pages.

This drive back to medievalism, which characterized so much of Christian left politics in the early decades of the twentieth century, was accomplished without any recognition of the central characteristics of much of that period – the subjection to serfdom of the overwhelming majority of the population. This type of existence becomes insignificant to the neo-medievalist when compared to society's stand against usury and the near total regulation of trade.

The fifth report was Temple's economic bible. The most significant of the report's findings was that the industrial system as it is constituted 'makes it exceedingly difficult to carry into practice the principles of Christianity. Its faults are not accidental... They are expressions of certain deficiencies deeply rooted in the nature of that order itself.'[13]

This was the refrain on which Temple expended so much of his breath over the next two decades. He would cite passages from a handful of reports, all written by the same people, on the – to him – 'troublesome' nature of profits and competition. Tracts against usury, of when a small rate of interest could be charged and when it would not be justifiable to charge interest, flowed from Temple's pen. Readers could be forgiven in thinking that licences for credit rates would be issued by order of the Church Assembly and offenders dragged before specially convened church courts.

The legacy

Temple's campaigning in the inter-war years deserves significant pluses as well as minus marks. The economic nonsense that Temple propagated fortunately never got past Clement Attlee, Labour's post-war prime minister, and played little part in Labour's 1945 economic strategy. It nevertheless delivered a bitter harvest when Labour was weakest, helping to lay the basis for a left political culture that was, by the 1970s, deeply hostile to the role markets could and should play in a modern economy. Decades of asserting the evils of competition made it much easier for escapist politics to divert attention from where the electorate wished the political debate to be. Wild utopianism replaced the hard graft involved in deciding at what level taxation should be set, the optimum size of a public sector and how best income can be redistributed to the least advantaged while, at one and the same time, maintaining an economy that is more dependent on international trade than those of most of our competitors.

Like so many people, Temple was a paradox. He was guilty of proposing policies without taking into account the impact on the poorest, yet he would spend so much of the rest of his time promoting their interests as he saw them. This allowed him to assert that the market economy or, as he preferred to call it, competition 'is simply organised selfishness...and a great deal has been said in praise of competition, and most of it is rubbish.'[14]

Temple in fact held this view despite what he saw as the superiority of the market system in the creation of wealth and its distribution. Writing towards the end of his life, the Archbishop judged that capitalism had

> certainly given the mass of the people a higher standard of life – a larger enjoyment of material goods – than any previous system [and] it seems nearly certain that no other system would have developed so rapidly or so far the new powers conferred by modern science.[15]

Yet at the same time, in 1942, Temple returned to his favourite subject. The 'profit motive should never be allowed to predominate...when it comes first in the determination of economic and industrial activity...it [is] to be condemned'.[16] For good measure, the Archbishop then pronounced on credit – another golden leitmotif: 'it should now be regarded as improper for any private person or corporation to issue new credit...I should like...to see banks limited in their lending powers to sums equivalent to that which depositors have entrusted to them.'[17] In the explosion in the media following these statements, the Archbishop added, disingenuously, that of course he was speaking as a private individual. What private individual, I wonder, is invited to a packed Albert Hall to deliver his or her views on credit? But against these absurd comic fantasies must be placed the other side of William's contribution to public life.

There was, for example, a hugely wholesome and massively positive side to Temple's campaigning. In the decisive decades of the new century, Labour was jockeying for recognition as a legitimate political party in the state. The role of Christian Socialism from the CSU stable, and later Temple himself, with his magical presence and evident holiness, should not be underestimated here. Their public stance on issues, close as they so often were to Labour's stance, helped give the new party the respectability it desperately needed to break through the class ceiling of snobbery which operated in British politics.

There was too an overlap between the Christian left, which was larger then, and Labour Party activists and rank-and-file. Many of the former group were part of the backbone of the local intelligentsia which generally found a welcome in Labour politics. Here were individuals who brought to the party's councils a clearly considered moral position. That morality should matter in politics was a political stance for which Temple was such an effective apostle.

There is also the important political role Temple played despite espousing such doubtful economic theories, and for which I believe we all stand in his debt. Temple's life's work helped to sweep many non-Labour voters into an enthusiasm for building the New Jerusalem that Mr Attlee planned. 'A people's war should give way to a people's peace' was the essence of Temple's last political campaign. Yet I cannot help feeling that Temple helped achieve this goal despite what he said. It was how he lived that was so important. So perhaps the last comment might therefore go to one of those prelates whom the young turks in Temple's campaign so loved to kick. Writing in the early nineteenth century, Archbishop Sumner observed: 'Men, in every state, are less induced to change of their present habit by reason, than by example.'[18] It is in the example of Temple's own holy living, from his consuming belief that the greatest force for change in this world came from the impact of a Christian life acting through individuals, that his lasting attraction and importance lies.

4

William Temple: a political evaluation

Introduction

William Temple is understandably written about in laudatory terms. Yet his political impact is rarely considered. Until the Second World War Temple's views were based on a Victorian idea of the inevitability of progress. Only when he was living through a world war for a second time did Temple accept that human affairs are not to be rationally understood. His political failure fully to comprehend self-interest's role in politics, calling to its importance in one of his best passages, was mirrored by much of the left in the mistaken belief that it was somehow a proper moral outlook. In this respect, he was unlike his lifelong friend R. H. Tawney, who always stressed the fallen side of human nature, as well as humankind's ability unexpectedly to act altruistically. Only recently has the British left tried to negotiate itself away from this inadequate view about human nature.

In making the Church central to the political debate, Temple believed it possible to counter the world's secularizing influences. Despite the nobility of this effort, Temple does not present himself as having a clear view of where power lies, of the best way of trying to influence the exercise of it, or of how to adapt his own role as he moved upwards in the Establishment. Yet he was paradoxically one of the outstanding figures in twentieth-century Britain and one of the few clerics to have a mass appeal which stretched across the class divide.

Among William Temple's achievements should be listed that he was, without doubt, the outstanding religious figure in Britain during the first half of the twentieth century. He was, as has already been remarked, a major player in helping to forge the new political consensus which Paul Addison suggested dropped into Attlee's lap in 1945.[1] Furthermore, along with George Bell he did more than anyone else in the country to advance a world-wide union between the reformed Catholic and Protestant churches.

Significant though these achievements are, Temple achieved a great deal more. He was primarily a devout, jovial and saintly person. He was also a Christian politician of great talent who in the process of being politically active 'significantly modified an Anglican interpretation of England', as John Kent, one of his biographers, claims.[2] His main purpose was, however, to maintain English Christianity in a central position within political society, and standing where we do in history we can see the lack of success in achieving this primary objective. But this failure was not for want of trying. We cannot make sense of his major campaigns unless we realize that his overriding objective was to counter the marginalization of Christianity in British society. But this political strategy was developed in stages: first in the campaign to reform the Church of England's position vis-à-vis the state; then by establishing powerful pressure groups which would advance his socio-political objectives; and last by his ecumenical activities.

The Life and Liberty movement

By the time Temple had come of age ecclesiastically, the threat to the established Church's position came not from disestablishment campaigns but from the increased secularization of life which made the established Church seem at best old-fashioned and at worst irrelevant. Moreover, many of the younger clergy had been radicalized by their experience at the front during

World War I. The braver the priest and the closer to the front he went, the clearer became two lessons. The first was that, despite the Church being established – running church schools, fighting over how religious knowledge should be taught in state schools, putting enormous resources behind the Sunday School movement, organizing church youth clubs and church societies and the like – the knowledge soldiers had of the Christian faith was distinguished largely by its absence. The second was that the form of services upon which most clergy had been raised and which they in turn offered – matins and evensong – was pathetically limited for the contemporary circumstances of war and of imminent death on a mass scale. Anglican clergy looked enviously at their Roman Catholic colleagues, whose behaviour met the hour. What these Catholic priests did, in forgiving sins and administering the bread of life, seemed wholly in tune with the hour and with what Roman Catholic soldiers understood and expected. How could the established Church, which was in so many eyes linked to the privileges held by the upper classes, begin to speak either to the private who was likely to die in the mud or to his grieving family at home? What part too could this unreformed established Church play in constructing a fairer society after the war in which Christian values were taught, understood and lived out in everyday life?

To Temple, the answer was 'not very much'. Hence the urgency for church reform, for which, as we have seen, he worked full-time with the Life and Liberty campaign. Some of those in the campaign believed Temple sold them short. But that is to misunderstand or to ignore Temple's political objective here. It was not a matter of theology for him that the Church should be disestablished. There were certain circumstances where that might be necessary. What was required was a degree of independence which would allow a reordering of the liturgy without parliamentary interference, for example, so making services understandable to those privates who were fortunate enough to return home. There was an equal need for the Church to have the maximum freedom of opportunity to promote a social theology which was in direct contrast to Victorian individualism. Temple saw, somewhat cannily, that the established position offered opportunities of playing a major political role in British society. That political advantage was not to be unthinkingly surrendered. To others in the Life and Liberty campaign, disestablishment was an ideological objective, although the ideology was dressed up in theological garments. Not so with Temple, who was ever pragmatic in his political approach.

The campaign, which resulted in the 1919 Enabling Act, was, as we have seen, a mixture of good old-fashioned rabble-rousing combined with some skilful lobbying. But whereas most of the hierarchy wished for modest reform, the radical elements of Life and Liberty wanted disestablishment. A middle position was sought and offered: the formation of the Church Assembly.

Copec

It very soon became obvious to Temple that this Assembly was not going to be the body which would reposition the Church in the eyes of the masses. Nor was its composition one which would willingly embrace Temple's socio-political views, particularly as earlier in his career he loved shocking people by calling his ideas socialist. Hence the switch in Temple's efforts, of largely ignoring the reformed institutions of the established Church he did so much to create, and seeking alternative vehicles through which he could campaign.

The first such vehicle went under the name of the Conference on Christian Politics, Economics and Citizenship – or Copec for short – and was held in Birmingham between 5 and 12 April 1924. The way this group went about its work, and the seriousness of the care it gave to its reports, set standards which few church conferences have since met. It is certainly the first of two major twentieth-century Christian Socialist initiatives.

(The second, the Oxford Conference, which was organized in 1937, was part of an international initiative.)

Temple was clearly the star attraction and the great driving force in the Life and Liberty campaign. In Copec, the intellectual work was much more shared than it had been in the Life and Liberty campaign. The organizing genius, as well as the intellectual clout, of Copec came from Joe Oldham, one of the two great lay bureaucrats of the twentieth century (the other was William Patten). And here we see one of Temple's political abilities: he found it easy to work with whoever was the most talented advocate of the reforms he favoured.

Copec's council of 350 members, with Temple as chairman, was established in 1920. Twelve commissions produced book-length reports which John Kent views as being much more important than the conference itself.[3] It is certainly true that rarely has a church – or a political party come to that – made such careful preparation before moving towards drafting a manifesto. The reports dealt with *The Nature of God and His Purpose in the World, Education, The Home, The Relation of the Sexes, Leisure, The Treatment of Crime, International Relations, Christianity and War, Industry and Property, Politics and Citizenship, The Social Function of the Church* and *Historical Illustrations of the Social Effects of Christianity*. These titles tell their own story of the extensive preparation and of how widely 'the world and Christianity' was interpreted. The books sum up one side of the social thinking which had gone on in the English churches since the beginning of the nineteenth century, and nothing like them has appeared since.[4] *Industry and Property* was perhaps the most impressive. But then this report followed closely the line of argument developed in the Archbishop's report, *Christianity and Industrial Problems*. This commission had among its members the most radical bishops, Charles Gore, F. D. Woods and J. A. Kepthorn, as well as George Lansbury, Albert Mansbridge – the initiator and organizing power behind the Workers' Educational Association – and R. H. Tawney. Also, a junior member, but only in terms of his age, was George Bell. The central ideas in both of these reports and the distorting effect they had on the radical debate in this country will be considered later.

A world stage

Copec did not provide the political breakthrough for which Temple had hoped. He met with some success in influencing the debate within the Church, although Temple rarely fooled himself that church gatherings by themselves led to much political influence, let alone power. Temple's main objective could not have been clearer: it was for the Church to influence political developments in the direction of the social Christianity in which he believed so passionately. Yet Temple never discovered the means of using the Copec reports, and others like them, as a battering ram into the general political debate. He didn't, for example, begin to appreciate the advantage the House of Lords gives to the bench of bishops, who could have been given individual responsibility for each of these reports, thereby making them part of the parliamentary agenda. Nor did he seek to give ownership of the reports to the Church Assembly.

Copec, and later the conference at Malvern, took on the role once occupied by the great Victorian missionary societies and campaigns. Each of these bodies was established in response to the failure of activists to shift the hierarchy fast enough in their direction. Temple's political method was to organize outside campaigns so as to strengthen his position on the inside, but he was already one of the most powerfully placed insiders. His strategy puzzles me. Temple was for much of this time either viewed as the natural successor to the top church position at Canterbury or, for the briefest period, the occupier of that very office. Yet he appears unable to cease being the talented outsider wishing to control the inside.

Commenting on the Church's involvement in politics, Temple remarked that when individuals demanded that the Church should do something they usually meant that the bishops should say something. Saying something was only important to Temple if it could lead to action. Many of the societies of the inter-war years missed how serious Temple was in this respect. Meeting them provided Temple with an intellectual relaxation, just as lesser mortals would attempt a crossword puzzle. Debates within the Christendom Group, for example, about the evils of credit and the need to re-establish a medieval hegemony, were entered into with a spirit of adventure. But what Temple most needed from any group was a clear line of action. With so many of these church groups this was the last thing that they were ever able to deliver, and Temple failed to marshal support for such a strategy.

So, ironically, Temple found himself increasingly saying rather than doing things. This inability to control events can be measured by the way Temple moved from group to group, as if it was a failure of organization which led to Temple's lack of influence.

As the 1920s became the 1930s, Temple's activities become increasingly frenetic. The church pressure groups were clearly failing to have the effect which Temple demanded of them. As the Church's influence on contemporary events and thinking continued to wane, Temple asked what could provide an alternative bulwark against its growing marginalization in contemporary culture. His answer was the Ecumenical Movement.

Temple was clearly a figure of importance in this movement, but I wonder if he was the towering figure which he is all too often painted. The glory – if this activity is to be so described – was shared. The missionary societies began it all 100 years ago. Randall Davidson gave a friendly nudge to the sickly infant. The first dominant and charismatic figure was Söderblom, the Swedish primate (appointed by the Swedish king, who overruled the Swedish Church's own favourite candidate).

The churches, rather heroically but nevertheless mistakenly, believed that, had they been more united, they might have prevented the outbreak of war in 1914. It was this feeling that Söderblom kept alive during the grotesque mass slaughter which occurred over the next four years and built upon with such effect as the armed hostilities ceased. The Church might prevent the outbreak of yet another major armed conflict between the great powers if only it could concentrate its strength into a single body. Now is not the place to record more details of these early events or of the first grand convention Söderblom called in Sweden in the mid-1920s. All that needs to be said is that the Ecumenical Movement was under the protection of two wings. The first, Life and Work, concerned itself with the immediate politics in which the world found itself. It was because of Söderblom's dominance, and his championing of George Bell as heir apparent, that Temple never gained much influence here, despite the fact that it was the natural home for his talents. The rallying cry of Life and Work was, after all, that united social action did not first require theological agreement. Temple's efforts instead went into Faith and Order, the body concerned with attempts to forge a unity of dogma. But even here Temple was up against a formidable opponent. A. C. Headlam, Bishop of Gloucester, was chairman of the Church's foreign relations committee, the body through which it issued official statements.[5]

It was therefore in response to his failure to control the established organs through which church unity was being attempted that Temple once again found himself looking elsewhere. The proposal for a World Council of Churches must have appeared to Temple like the cavalry charging over the hill. Here was a political vehicle he could begin to fashion in his own image. And that fashioning was from the purest of motives. It offered two important political opportunities: the Church would gain an international platform to draw attention to the way it believed the deteriorating international situation should be countered, while at home a united front offered a possibility of acting as a safe island surrounded by an apparently ever-rising sea of social and culture pluralism.

Temple's efforts were not totally consumed by the new era of church international politics. The home front mattered too. In 1942 the Malvern Conference aimed at picking up the debate where Copec left it. Temple was anxious that the Church should play a more effective political role after the war than it had achieved in 1918. Within these organizations ideas were debated, and from their membership support groups for Temple were established. Some active politicians could testify to the importance of both these activities.

The New Testament holds out two models of political action. The first is the light on the hill, beckoning and judging a fallen world. The other is the yeast which, when permeating the unleavened lump, loses its own separate identity, but has a fundamental effect on the whole process. I suspect that Temple never clearly made up his mind which approach to adopt, or thought clearly about where power lies in the political process and the best way of influencing, let alone capturing, it. It may be wrong to read it as an article of faith that a single approach is right whatever the circumstances. Confronted with the evil of Nazism, a policy of day-to-day engagement to ensure its destruction is the most pressing need. But once the goal was within striking distance – and with the Americans in the war it became a matter of time before the Axis powers were defeated – humanity needed a beacon holding out hope for a new tomorrow.

But that new tomorrow can only successfully be shaped by an effective political strategy. Temple, while appearing ever busy, never seemed to be clear as to what role he was adopting and why. Nor did he evaluate properly the balance between the insider and the outsider, or adapt his stance as his own position in the political elite changed. Unlike all of his predecessors, Temple marginalized his role in the Lords. Yet he could have built up a commanding position here in one house of the legislature which then had far more political clout than it enjoys today. Indeed, most commentators now seem ignorant of the strategic position the Lords often played in English politics up to and including the Second World War. Cold draughty halls in Malvern are the place for those who are outsiders, not for those whose position gives them a pivotal position in the legislature.

The balance sheet

For anyone who has never met or heard of this prince of the Church, Adrian Hastings' essay[6] provides several clues as to why he was so popular, why he was clearly loved by working people who would never step inside a church except for rites of passage, and why he commanded world-wide attention.

But the more one appreciates the comprehensiveness of Temple's influence and following, the more difficult it is not to be critical of his political approach and achievements. Few politicians, and certainly not church leaders, commanded a comparable following. All his efforts were directed at countering the growth of a secularization which marginalized and undermined the influence of Christianity.

Adrian Hastings observes that, despite all his efforts, Temple lacked direction until he was in his forties and firmly ensconced at York. But it is difficult to see that at York Temple thought through what his best political strategy might be. Hastings believes that not only did Temple never quite grow up, but he never really wanted to do so. Perhaps that schoolboy laugh which stayed with him until the end is significant.

Part of growing up to become a serious political figure, as well as an effective reformer, is a willingness to understand how those organizations actually work which will be on the receiving end of one's reforming zeal. This requires concentrated hard work. Despite all the hours Temple spent labouring for the Kingdom, he was singularly unwilling to put in this kind of work. His mother once revealingly remarked that, while William had a hundred new ideas at breakfast, he would have forgotten them by lunchtime.

When appointed in 1910 to Repton, Temple declared that his objective was to revolutionize the school and show how to break a crucial link in Britain's cycle of privilege. What happened once Temple took up his position? Not very much, other than the change of a music master. Hastings' comments on this aspect of Temple's character deserve quoting in full.

> I believe that Repton episode is far more of a parable for Temple's whole career than is usually admitted. I suspect that when he helped mount the 'Life and Liberty' campaign with such ringing, revolutionary words, he had little more idea of how the Church of England worked than in 1910 he had about public schools. I also doubt whether he had any real sense of the plight of the industrial poor or what they would be up against when he called Copec or endeavoured to negotiate in the latter stages of the miners' strike, and I doubt whether he had any very sharp sense as to what was going on in Germany in the 1930s, or, say, the British war time policy of obliteration bombing.[7]

It would be a grave distortion to end on a negative note, although here the air is heavy with irony. While Temple failed in his major objective of keeping the Church at the centre of contemporary life and culture, he personally played an important role in changing the direction of the political debate at home and abroad. Although he was not the only cleric to advocate social reform – Bell did so – he was by far the most important exponent of the view that ordinary people deserved a better deal.

In this he was far more effective than the Labour leadership – with, perhaps, the sole exception of the trade union leader turned coalition government minister, Ernest Bevin – in conveying what should and could happen. Those of us who are war-time babies, or who were born since, owe him a debt for helping to make our lives so different from the lives of those who grew up in the inter-war years. Temple raised people's hopes and encouraged them not to settle for another round of the 1930s. That Germany was not the rogue elephant of the post-war period owes something to Temple. It was, however, Bell who played the more important role. Yet Temple's view on the role that justice should play in international affairs had its effect too.

Conclusion

Temple died on 26 September 1944. His death brought to an abrupt end the role the established Church and its leader had played in domestic politics for well over 1,000 years. From now on, the decline in influence which Temple had devoted his life to reversing continued remorselessly.

Fifty years ago, a 16-year-old lad switched on the wireless (as it was then called) at the London wharf where he worked and heard of Temple's death. Eric James will not have been the only one to burst into tears on hearing that news. Few public figures secured, as Temple did, such a hold over people's affections. But Temple's end was characteristically one of humour. The day after his funeral his ashes were buried near his father's grave at Canterbury. Mrs Temple noticed that the urn was likely to fall over as the earth was replaced. Down into the grave went the undertaker to repair the damage, only to find that he was unable to scramble out unaided. There was the real possibility of Mrs Temple and Temple's secretary being pulled into the pit as they attempted to haul up the obedient undertaker.

After 63 years of near-constant effort, Temple had burnt himself out. Richard Hooker observed: 'Ministers of good things are like torches, a light to others, waste and destruction to themselves.' Here was a torch the like of which we are unlikely to see blazing again in our lifetime.

5

Christianity and Social Order: *the book and the nation*

———•◦•———

William Temple's only recorded failure in public speaking came when he was addressing a group of students on the question of unbelief. He conceded afterwards that, never having suffered doubts himself, it was somewhat incongruous for him to speak on such a subject and to an audience that knew more than he did about the topic he was discussing.

This response by Temple is less than totally honest. That Temple never doubted the existence of God has to be appreciated. It governed his every action, public as well as private. He did, however, initially express doubts on some lesser topics. His early questioning of the Virgin Birth was fortunately quickly dispelled when it looked as though such questioning would act as a bar to his ordination. And Temple's views on the Resurrection likewise became orthodox. The only time he offered up any questioning on this score was after hauling his huge frame up a steep hill with young colleagues. At the summit he explained his relief in never believing in the physical resurrection of the flesh.

Temple's life was about communicating his central belief in the truth of Christianity. Moreover, it was a truth which could not be confined to the private activities of individuals. Its rule was as relevant to the thinking of public figures and actions as it was accepted in the confessional.

The big influences

Temple was the inheritor of the Victorian concept of a national Church, an ideal which, as the nineteenth century moved through its final decades, became an increasingly less accurate description of reality. But it is easy to see why Temple subscribed to this view. As a small boy, he played in the grounds of Fulham Palace, even thinking up a marriage ceremony so as to 'wed' the little daughter of the local vicar. It was to the palace that he brought his school friends from Colet Court and later Rugby. His Balliol companions stayed at Lambeth Palace. Up to young adulthood, Temple's home had always been a palace.

As Bishop of Exeter and then of London, and finally as Archbishop of Canterbury, William's father was at the centre of the Establishment. Frederick, his father, was active in the Lords and diligent at court. It is hard now to conjure up the central position the Anglican Church once played in the life of the nation. It still holds this position in orchestrating national pageants such as coronations. But these gala performances were then merely the outward visible sign of considerable influence, and of a political power wielded beyond the gaze of the masses.

There is that staggering entry in George Bell's life of Randall Davidson, the successor archbishop to William's father, which records the Prime Minister seeking out the Primate to discuss key political matters of the day which had yet to be broached with those colleagues sitting alongside him at the Cabinet table. It was as though Lambeth provided the necessary lubrication enabling government to function more smoothly and effectively.

This was a world in which William lived, breathed and grew up, but the way William began to view this world was shaped by three intellectual giants. The first, as we have seen in the previous essays, was his father who, while headmaster of Rugby School, was known as 'the just beast'. The second was the founder of modern Rugby, Thomas Arnold. The third great influence was Edward Caird, who was Master of Balliol when William went up as an undergraduate. Frederick's choice was for William to go to his old college. 'Take anything you can get at Balliol. Better Balliol with nothing than Trinity with an exhibition.'[1]

Temple's approach to education was one which made an indelible mark on his son. So too did his approach to truth and knowledge. Reason had a fundamental role in establishing truth, but it was not reason run wild. Reason had still to be pitted against conscience. Temple senior was nothing if not a true inheritor of the Reformation in this respect. Frederick also saw the clearest link between religion and morality and maintained that it was the study of history to which we must turn in order to see those moral principles by which we should live.

Temple junior adopted this approach and emphasized various parts of it. Writers have expressed surprise that Temple's philosophical works began not at the centre – with God – but at the circumference, tracing a path towards that centre. But, as we have seen, William never had doubts about God's existence, so there should be no surprise in his concern primarily with how the world related to God.

The influence of Dr Arnold is also there for everyone to behold. It affected William's churchmanship. While a national Church had to be comprehensive, Temple never quite went to the lengths of his mentor in advocating membership for everyone, barring only 'Jew' and 'Infidel'. And again, while Temple drew back from believing that social progress was coterminous with extending the Kingdom, he sympathized with Arnold's view that humanity's kingdoms are meant to become providences of that greater Kingdom.

It was in respect of his social sympathy that William gained much from these two austere headmasterly figures. Arnold gave his sympathy for the poor a distinct cutting edge. The free market was to be attacked. Industry must be brought to book for regarding workers as mere hands. The Church was to be reprimanded for never daring 'to speak boldly to the great but contenting itself with lecturing the poor'.

So far so good. But William's mind thought in systems. That was his training, and loose sympathy for the poor was no substitute for a rigorous framework governed by Christian principles. Such an approach would be intellectually acceptable, as it would favour the poor. These were pre-Orwellian days, when the cry of a fairer society could be equated with raising the status of the most humble.

Iremonger, the official biographer, quotes Temple as saying that intellectually he got over his measles at Rugby, adding that once Temple had decided upon his philosophical framework 'There was little shifting in the premises'.[2] There may have been no significant movement in the premises upon which William's life's work was based, but the way it was to be presented did most markedly change, and here we need to consider the third great figure influencing William.

Caird's influence lay in giving William a political ideology, albeit one cast in religious terms. Caird was one of the most important second-generation Idealists who, like the founder of English Idealism, T. H. Green, saw his political concerns arising naturally from his Idealistic philosophy. For William, who possessed a frame of mind that longed to be able to express how the world related to his consciousness, Caird's political philosophy proved to be the greatest of attractions.

Theological framework

There were few disappointments in Temple's life. A childless marriage and the loss of the Ellerton Theological Essay Prize almost complete the list. Circumstances raised him in optimism, so much so that, for most of his life, he seemed unable to take account of the darker side of human nature. In every sense, he was the beneficiary of late-Victorian confidence and wealth. Yet for someone who spent so much of his energies opposing the growth of secular influence, he became one of the main propagandists of its central idea: the inevitability of progress.

Addressing students not long before a world war that would kill millions, Temple gave an extraordinarily optimistic account of human history.

> Remembering that the world has progressed a good deal since the earliest ages that we know, and progressed in love more perhaps than in any other quality, we shall find that it may be true that the whole world is moving forwards forever under the impulse of the infinite love of God to a more and more adequate return of that love.

Eric James has said that it helps to judge a person by knowing who their favourite poet is. Temple's was unquestionably Browning. While President of the Oxford Union he published an essay on the poet, and Joseph Fletcher has Temple asserting that Browning's 'Death in the Desert' is the best commentary on the fourth Gospel.[3] Temple's attachment to the poet was so great that during his ten-day honeymoon he read Browning aloud in the evenings. Mrs Temple's reaction, regrettably, is not recorded. In Browning, Temple found someone who not only extolled the role of reason, but whose poems were dominated by images of truth and beauty.

Temple, writing to a friend while still an undergraduate, explained, 'The doctrine of the Incarnation, permanently present in its purity to Browning, is hopelessly mauled by every clergyman who touches it'. More importantly, the view of the world depicted by Browning was one which Temple brought to his theology. Within such a framework, it was therefore doubly hazardous for Temple to espouse for much of his life the importance of the Incarnation almost to the total exclusion of other doctrines.

The Incarnation is essentially a doctrine of hope. Here is God coming as his Son on earth, signifying all that is good and the importance to which God attaches to all that goes on in his domain. In late 1937, Temple writes the introduction to the Church's doctrine report, where he observes that the theology of the Incarnation 'tends to be Christocentric metaphysic'.

And in all ages there is a need 'for the fresh elaboration of such a scheme of thought or map of life as seen in the light of the revelation of Christ'. That new map he provided in *Christianity and Social Order*, though by the time he wrote this great little book Temple's theological moorings were breaking loose.

Iremonger's judgement has been cited earlier, that William's thinking was quickly all of a piece, and that once the great intellectual architecture had been put in place 'there was little shifting' of the main structure. This statement remained true to the end of his life, but only because in his sustained work Temple ceased to present accurately what his actual position was.

Christianity and Social Order followed what was now William's well-established argumentative order. But the graceful movement of the episcopal swan gave no hint of the sheer intellectual excitement, not to say turmoil, below the waterline as this great human 'beast' thrashed around in tides that made a nonsense of much of his life's thinking.

The writing of *Christianity and Social Order* was completed quickly and followed the lines he wanted to emerge from the 1941 Malvern Conference. Half the book is taken up with a defence of the Church 'interfering' – Temple's choice of word – in politics. But what a concession for someone who was essentially arguing a medieval cosmology to justify the Church's right to be active in public life.

It is only towards the middle of the book that the serious argument begins, with Temple moving into full gear. Here are passages so central to Temple's beliefs that he might have written them in his sleep – William, after all, claimed to do his thinking then. In 11 pages Temple manages to summarize all the main arguments about God and his purpose, together with the dignity, tragedy and destiny of humankind. Many a rain forest could have been saved if church propagandists had settled to reprint these few pages of Temple's instead of producing a vast range of bulky and perhaps unread tomes on the self-same theme.

These 11 pages, in addition, also manage to contain one of the best explanations of original sin, together with the role of self-interest in public affairs.

> When we open our eyes as babies we see the world stretching out around us; we are in the middle of it; all proportions and perspectives in what we see are determined by the relation – distance, height, and so forth – of the various visible objects to ourselves. This will remain true of our bodily wisdom as long as we live…the same thing is true at first of our mental and spiritual vision. Some things hurt us…we call them bad. Some things please us…we call them good…so each of us takes his place in the centre of his own world. But I am not the centre of the world, or the standard of reference as between good and bad; I am not, and God is. In other words, from the beginning I put myself in God's place. This is original sin.[4]

Temple believed that, by education, we could make our self-centredness less compelling. Education, by its very nature, could widen our horizons and so free us partially from original sin. 'But complete deliverance can be effected only by the winning of my whole heart's devotion, the total allegiance of my will – and this only the Divine Love disclosed by Christ in His Life and Death can do.'[5]

Temple is equally decisive on self-interest and woolly-minded left-wing politicians. He cites what ought to be the most quoted of all the many sentiments ever to flow from his pen.

> A statesman who supposes that a mass of citizens can be governed without appeal to their self-interest is living in a dreamland and is a public menace. The art of government in fact is the art of so ordering life that self-interest prompts what justice demands.[6]

That this passage is not that often quoted is in no small part due to the left-wing political correctness which Temple strangely did so much to promote in his other writings and speeches. It runs counter to his economic beliefs that were outlined in the previous essay. His stress on the evils of competition, for example, would have been much more powerful and relevant if this understanding of the central motive force self-interest plays in our lives had been given its full rein.

The primary principles

The traditional premises about God and how humankind's destiny and thereby freedom lies in seeking a permanent loving relationship with him give us what Temple calls the primary Christian social principles. Temple then considers what Christian social principles are derived from this starting point. In 1923, Temple listed four such principles: freedom, social fellowship, service and sacrifice. By 1942, these derivative principles are reduced to three – at the high point of the war against the Nazi aggressors, Temple surprisingly axes sacrifice.

History, his father had taught, delivered up moral principles. Temple's reading of the signs leads him very early to enunciate a system built around the primacy of the individual. That system which argued the sacredness of each individual swayed about in the intellectual climate of pre- and post-war Britain, reflecting sometimes the desolation into which the less fortunate of Britain were plunged during the inter-war years. As time went on, Temple's thinking assumed a much more individualistic stance.

Temple never accepted John Stuart Mill's perception that freedom was defined by the absence of any restraining force. People needed educating to know that choices were available and what might be their consequences. Until education had done its work,

> you can have no real freedom because until a man's whole personality has developed he cannot be free in his own life; he will not be capable of forming the ideal to satisfy his whole nature, and then setting himself steadily in the pursuit of it.

So freedom operates within a society and societies are run by states. The position of the state, and its relation to freedom, changes drastically in Temple's mode of thought.

In his earlier writings, the collectivist view is to the fore. 'A man has no right to have his talents developed,' writes Temple in 1905,

> apart from his intentions to devote them to the state, because his whole being is comprised in the fact that he is a member of the state...man is essentially and before all else a member of the state, and can only realise his egotistic ends by realising and living up to that membership.[7]

Over a decade and a half later, in *Mens Creatrix*, he still has the state in a dominant role. Here, Temple writes, 'liberty is control [of] the parts by the whole which they constitute'.[8]

A decisive shift occurs in Temple's concept of freedom at the time of the 1925 General Strike, or perhaps because of it. And in his private papers on the General Strike held at Lambeth Palace Library, Temple records that 'In the last resort there is both a right and a duty of resistance.'[9]

In the space of a little over two decades, Temple had moved from a collectivist to an individualist stance on freedom, and although it wasn't the kind of freedom that individualists propagated so successfully during the 1980s, it is difficult to maintain, as Temple himself did, that he had rid himself of intellectual measles while a schoolboy in Rugby. So Temple is well placed to respond to the rise of Fascism. In 'The Freedom for which We Fight', Temple writes: 'Man...has a status which is independent of any earthly society and has a higher dignity than any state can confer.'

Spencer, who cites this quotation in his article on Temple, draws the reader's attention to the way Temple is now opening the way for 'a religious basis for his political theory'.[10] That basis is for the individual's pre-eminence on God's love for each and every one of us. What is more surprising than any development in Temple's thought is that it is only in the 1930s, when he is Archbishop of York, that commentators feel that he is 'opening the way' for a religious basis for his political theory.

Freedom is by far and away the most important derivative principle. But what of the two other principles which Temple enunciates, fellowship and service? With a flurry, Temple observes, 'man is naturally an incurably social animal', adding,

> no man is fitted for an isolated life; everyone has needs which he cannot supply for himself; but he needs not only what his neighbours contribute to the equipment of his life but their actual selves as the complement of his own.[11]

Elsewhere, in considering the working of democracy, Temple makes out the case for intermediate or countervailing centres of power to the state. Thankfully, Temple had drunk from the same cup as that eccentric but brilliant Mirfield monk, Neville Figgis.[12] Here, that framework is used to fashion how individuals operate outside the family. While the state is crucial to the way we live our lives, most people do not relate to it. Indeed, most of us sensibly do not give it a second thought. Yet it sets a framework of law within which much human activity takes place.

Our lives, in contrast, are made by the organizations to which we belong; school, church, political party, trade union, darts team, sports club, gym – the list is almost endless. 'Now,' observes Temple, 'actual liberty is the freedom which many enjoy in these various social units.'[13]

One cannot help thinking that William's father's influence is strongly present here in his son's thinking. There is also an element of skating on thin ice – a dangerous activity at the best of times, let alone for someone of Temple's weight – in arguing that fellowship is derivative from the primary principles enunciated earlier. History, however, would certainly teach the wisdom of arguing the importance of voluntary associations.

A similar criticism can be made of the third derivative principle: service. Let Temple speak for himself.

The combination of Freedom and Fellowship as principles of social life issues in the obligation of Service. No-one doubts this in so far as it concerns the individual. Whatever our practice may be, we all give lip-service to this principle.[14]

Immediately, Temple is emphasizing the importance of voluntary service: how much we depend on it, why we need it, and so on. But a deliberative principle? The argument then switches in the space of a line to work as a form of service. Again, it is clearly necessary. History teaches that. But a derivative principle?

If these few pages lack the rigour once promised for them, they pack a particularly effective political punch. Service should not be undertaken at the expense of a person's major responsibility: to his family, only then to his neighbours, and then to the local community, and so on in this order. It is seldom that anyone can render a service directly to humankind as a whole. We serve humankind by serving those parts of it with which we are closely connected. And our narrower loyalties are likely to be more intense than the wider, and therefore call on more devotion and more strenuous effort. But we can and should check these keener, narrower loyalties by recognizing the prior claim in the context of the wider society's claims. So 'a man rightly does his best for the welfare of his own family, but must never serve his family in ways that injure the nation.'[15]

Here is an example of very valuable advice about which a community is constantly in need of being reminded. But if the reader finds it difficult to see how this is a derivative position there is little need to worry, for all of this sub-text is swept under the shadow of another great figure, Reinhold Niebuhr, the American theologian of German descent.

A mind in turmoil

Niebuhr, it is wrongly claimed, was obsessed with original sin. He only appears so as most writers at the time had never taken their story-telling beyond the first glimpse, let alone any munching of the apple. Temple first met Niebuhr as long ago as 1923, but it was not until the 1930s that Temple admitted that Niebuhr was disturbing him. Given all we know of Temple's self-confidence, this says much for Niebuhr.

Now, for the first time in *Christianity and Social Order*, in a few non-characteristic Temple passages, William begins to grapple with the limits of his near 50-year-old intellectual vision of how and why the world worked as it did. The debate is switched away from its primary market – addressing the nation – and becomes almost a personal dialogue with Niebuhr.

Here the strange hands of both Providence and a publisher are at work. Temple was constricted by a fine timetable. His volume was to be a companion to the Penguin Special George Bell had written.[16] The publisher was anxious to get it completed and in the shops.

While publishing timetables have their place in the great scheme of things, perhaps greater weight ought to be given to the message rather than to the medium. But if Temple had fought for time he might never have had the energy to finish the draft manuscript. The removal vans were seen once again at Bishopthorpe in York. This time they headed south to the Primacy of All England and the onslaught of the great German bombing brigades.

Almost as soon as the Temples reached Canterbury, the bombs fell to greet them and in the process killed many local people. The Temples' residence at Canterbury was the old palace that Frederick had rebuilt by the cathedral. All the workmen restoring the palace lost either a relative or their possessions, or both, in these bombings. In London the Temples lived at Lambeth, a place from which the previous archbishop had long since decamped for life at the Athenaeum. Archbishop Lang, Temple's predecessor, greeted with disbelief the news that his successor and wife were intending to live in the ruin which once boasted a postal address as a palace.

So there was intense pressure on Temple to publish, and publish quickly. He was as anxious as ever to influence the outcome of post-war reconstruction. But the text, brief as it is, no longer reflected what Temple believed. By 1937, Niebuhr's approach was offering a more appropriate guide to our activities as we journey from the circumference of Temple's philosophical model towards God at the centre. It was in that year that volumes for the Oxford Conference, as it was called, were published. Perhaps Joe Oldham – the genius behind the event – or luck ensured that Temple's and Niebuhr's essays followed each other in Volume IV (*Christian Faith and the Common Life*) of the 'Church, Community and State' Oxford Conference of 1937.[17]

Only very late in life was Temple's optimism punctured by the overwhelming pressure of world events, and then only when Britain was about to begin actively fighting for survival against Nazi totalitarianism. In an article published in 1939, and which Adrian Hastings admits to be almost too painful for him to read, Temple appeared to overturn a lifetime's stance and belief.[18] To me it is one of William's most persuasive pieces of work. At last the dark side of human nature was allowed to be represented properly on life's canvas. Here Temple turns his back on a belief that human reason could always make sense of the world.

> We have to face this tormented world, not as offering a means to its coherence in thought and its harmony in practice, but as challenging it in the name and power of Christ crucified and risen; we shall not try to 'make sense' of everything, we shall openly proclaim that most things as they are have no sense in them at all. We shall not say that a Christian philosophy embraces all experience in a coherent and comprehensive scheme.[19]

Hastings, in his wonderfully challenging biographical essay on Temple, asserts that this article 'can best be dismissed as marginal to the interpretation of Temple's mind, a brief moment of lost confidence under the Angst of war'.[20] I am not so sure.

In contrast to Hastings, I believe it is the supreme moment in Temple's life when all the certainties that had guarded him from the cradle were overwhelmed by the sheer force of events. Furthermore, the article is not a one-off affair. In a letter he wrote to the philosopher Dorothy Emmet three years later, William, in a flash of brilliance, tries to bring the pieces together to present a dramatic new understanding of reason's role in explaining our existence.

> What we must completely get away from is the notion that the world as it now exists is a rational whole; we must think of its unity not by the analogy of the picture, of which all the parts exist at once, but by the analogy of a drama, where, if it is good enough, the full meaning of the first scene only becomes apparent with the final curtain; and we are in the middle of this. Consequently the world as we see it is strictly unintelligible. We can only have faith that it will become intelligible when the divine purpose, which is the explanation of it, is accomplished.[21]

William has ceased to be the great teacher, always brilliantly relaying to Church and nation the views he has inherited. For the first time, William's sheer quality as a thinker becomes apparent, and a thinker who has every bit of the courage that his father showed throughout his long life.

Conclusion

So why was *Christianity and Social Order*, which encapsulates Temple's youthful optimism and gives little to no hint of the intellectual turmoil into which the fight against Nazism plunged him, published in the form it was? There are, I think, two reasons. The first has already been alluded to: the matter of time. Temple was already working at a pace familiar to Mrs Thatcher while she was prime minister, but with little of a prime ministerial back-up staff. Letter after letter records that it is being written at the expense of his sleep.

There is that horrendous passage in *Sans Everything*,[22] reporting an agitated nurse in one of the old geriatric hospitals angrily shaking an old man on his deathbed. The man replies: 'It takes time to die, nurse, it takes time.' It also takes time to reconstruct, or rather build again, an intellectual framework and Temple, without knowing it, was near to his own deathbed.

There is another reason why *Christianity and Social Order* appeared in the form that it did. Its ideas, rooted in Edwardian England, conveyed a warmth and security which people rightly or wrongly associated with an age that they desperately wanted to revisit. Those ideas may have failed to deliver a land fit for heroes in 1918, but they could be used this time to carve out a better tomorrow, and that they certainly did. Whatever was going on in his head, William was not going to drop this political ball.

This was a salutary lesson, but one which would not have caused Frederick the least surprise. As a young, eager but bumptious member of the Bishop of London's household, William suggested what a better world it would be if the philosopher ruled. 'Foolish boy,' replied his elderly father, 'they do, but 500 years after their death.' William died on 26 October 1944. I somehow think that Frederick would not have been too surprised that his son cut that timescale down to less than 500 days. The great reforming 1945 Labour government was by then well into its stride, implementing many of the reforms for which William had so long campaigned and which he had helped make politically possible.

Part 2

A MAGNIFICENT ACT

Introduction

Unlike all the other heroes, George Kennedy Allen Bell's attractiveness stems from a single sacrificing action. I came to the Bell scene rather late. Many of those who knew him best had by then died. All the surviving friends and acquaintances stressed that Bell was untroubled by possibly being blocked from succeeding William Temple as Archbishop of Canterbury because of his great parliamentary speech against our country's obliteration bombing of German cities. While no one put this feeling in such clear terms, the tenor was clear: George was a saint and simply passed over worldly considerations when making his great stand.

This line might be true, but it troubled me. It made George a lesser person, I felt, if there had been no struggle, no worrying about career prospects and no anguish after the event. One person I was sure would have known what Bell really thought was Lancelot Mason, one of the two people who were the sons George and Hatty Bell never had. The other was, of course, Dietrich Bonhoeffer. But Lancelot was dead and there was no trace of any diary or papers. Still, Lancelot had a friend who was still alive – just. Lloyd Morrell had been a junior Bishop of Lewes in Bell's diocese of Chichester. So off I went to visit Bishop Morrell.

A retirement house had been bought that was approached by the steepest bank of steps I have ever experienced. The Bishop's sister had come to keep house. She had then had a stroke and the Bishop was immobile too and lived in a wheelchair. Their retirement home had become a prison. I put the question to my host: was Bell impervious to any punishment from the Establishment, for that is what everybody had told me. I said I was sure that he could overthrow the conventional wisdom, although he might believe it right to take this great secret to his grave. But if I was right, that Bell knew how severe the consequences would be but that telling the truth was greater than any worldly prize, didn't this cast Bell in even greater light?

There was no immediate reply from the Bishop, who appeared in some distress as he sat pondering in his wheelchair with his arms hanging over the sides. I repeated my question. Then, all of a sudden, the arms were activated and began banging against the wheels. The banging went on and ceased as abruptly as it had begun. The Bishop, whose face was now flushed, looked up. 'He cared every day of his life that no preferment came.' His face began draining of its redness.

Bell had been an apprentice at the very centre of the Establishment when he became Archbishop Davidson's chaplain. He would have known the rules about not rocking the boat at any time, but particularly in war. He made that great speech against our bombing policy knowing pretty well what the personal cost would be. Bell's talents may have been the reason he remained at Chichester (hardly a salt mine) for the remainder of his public career. But Bell wanted preferment for the opportunities this would offer him, cared about his rejection but believed he was right to tell a great uncomfortable truth. Such actions as Bell's live in people's hearts and inspire them to stretch themselves that little bit further towards perfection.

The outstandingly beautiful parish church at Thaxted had been reordered by Conrad Noel so that the worship conducted there might glorify God rather than the main players in the sanctuary. Extreme views always put me on the defensive, and never more than when high churchmanship is combined with a Trotskyite political philosophy. I was therefore initially hostile to Conrad Noel, who had the status of a local saint. But the more I learned about Conrad, the more I warmed to his defiance against a Church that even then was not overstocked with talent but that refused to make any, let alone the best, use of his extraordinary gifts. Thank God for the division of powers over appointments in the Church of England. The patron of Thaxted, Lady Warwick, is the third hero to step off the pages of the study of Bell and Noel. Long may such a system of protecting the awkward squad continue; at a minimum it makes life more exciting.

6

George Bell:
a uniquely consistent life

George Bell is at last receiving some of the attention he deserves.[1] In any circumstances he is a difficult person to get 'quite right'. In particular I want to oppose any view that there were distinct shifts in Bell's beliefs. To see Bell becoming more radical as he grappled with the turmoil of the 1930s is to mistake the man. Radicalism was inherent in Bell's views. While the events undoubtedly highlighted this radicalism, it was very much part of an extraordinarily coherent personal philosophy which was in place from the very outset of his career.

Speaking about George Kennedy Allen Bell presents a number of difficulties. There is, first, Bell's remarkable diffidence. Mary Joice, his secretary from 1942 until he retired as Bishop of Chichester in 1957, has commented that, had Bell ever achieved his ambition to write his autobiography, it would have been the first such book not to mention the main character.[2] As it is, very few records remain which directly touch upon his inner thoughts and struggles.

Not only was any self-publicity alien to Bell's nature, but he was also unlucky with his biographer. To pen an accurate portrait would require abilities similar to those that Bell himself displayed in his magisterial life of Archbishop Davidson. The person most likely to have been able to set Bell fully in the round was the outstanding church historian Dean Norman Sykes, but he died after completing some preliminary work. Ronald Jasper, who was invited to carry out the task, had published, among other works, a fine life of Arthur Headlam.[3] In that book, both subject and author were well matched. Jasper clearly warmed to his subject, whose interests were mainly clerical, and Headlam was ideally suited to Jasper's historiographical skills. In a number of ways, however, Jasper's study of Bell is unsatisfactory. Gordon Rupp's observation that Bethge's account rarely gets Bell 'quite right'[4] could be applied more generally to Jasper. The distorted death mask Jasper imposes on his subject is another factor making it difficult to put Bell into clear focus.

Time also counted against Bell. His mature years were lived out during the inter-war period, a period which still presents particular difficulties for succeeding generations who seek an accurate perspective. The slaughter rate was such that few families had remained unbroken by the extent of the carnage of World War I; five million Allied troops perished. Its continuing legacy was everywhere evident: in the disabled servicemen, in the fatherless children and their widowed mothers, and in the swathes of single women. A nation with such indelible scars inevitably reacted to events from Germany in a manner likely to be different from one which possessed no such collective memory. The change in perceptions between that generation born out of the First World War and its successors is perhaps best summed up in the meaning both sides give to the word 'appeasement'.[5] For many who lived to inherit the post-war world in 1918, appeasement was a noble ideal, compensating for past mistakes, while simultaneously guarding against nations unintentionally or unfairly stumbling again into a great conflict. For generations after the Second World War, the politics of appeasement were little short of treachery. It is significant that Jasper wrote at a time when criticism of appeasement was most rife, and the biography was published at a high point in the Cold War. There could hardly have been a more unfavourable period for a biography of Bell to have been written. Yet it is precisely through the maelstrom of changing appearances and perceptions of the inter-war years that Bell's work has to be considered.

Peering as we do at Bell as through a glass darkly, we must also recognize that his Christian faith smudges the lens a little further. Bell was undemonstrative. His Christian beliefs were so certain that they needed no questioning, and never had to be artificially introduced into any thinking or discussions. They were, for Bell, simply the great given. Bell lived out his Christian beliefs to a degree which can now only give rise to incomprehension in many quarters. If Bell was considered quaint by some contemporary critics, at least they understood the meaning attached to the language he used. In an age when Christian language acts as a barrier to rather than a purveyor of meaning, Bell's beliefs can today easily become a source of added confusion.

Lambeth apprenticeship

Personal history also plays a hand in adding to a series of all-pervasive paradoxes which characterizes George Bell's life and which again deflects from rather than facilitates any enquiry. Archbishop Davidson, almost at the end of his stewardship, writes to Bell as his senior chaplain in terms of their shared work, and attributes to Bell equal importance to what is accredited to Davidson. Few chaplains had developed this role in the way Bell had – indeed, later chaplains talk of how Bell personally shaped that role and the Archbishop's tribute stressed the 'uniqueness' of Bell's position at Lambeth.[6] Yet Jasper asserts that Davidson's estimation of Bell was one of characteristic generosity, and the debt owed by Bell to his Lambeth apprenticeship was undeniably greater than the debt owed by Lambeth to him.

Was the Archbishop being unduly generous? Here is another example of fate conspiring against an adequate accurate evaluation of Bell. A major reason why Davidson is seen by Jasper, and most other commentators, as such an all-pervasive figure is that they view him through Bell's eyes. If Davidson is viewed as one of the great figures of English public life, and indeed of Christianity in the early years of the twentieth century, it is in no small measure due to Bell's creation and promotion of that image. Yet, ironically, this success ultimately undermines Bell, who is forever obscured by the master whose mystique he did so much to create.

This is not the place to attempt a valuation of Bell's formative influence on Davidson while he was his chaplain. I wish rather to stress that Bell came to Lambeth with a theological and political framework already in place which, while developed over the following four decades, was never displaced by other sets of ideas. He did not become more radical as a result of events in the 1930s.

If the chaplaincy at Lambeth did not change or enlarge Bell's intellectual framework it clearly placed him in a position of great influence. It was a position which also brought him notice. Accepting the post was, however, a touch-and-go event. When Davidson asked Bell to be his chaplain during that August Bank Holiday in 1914 as Britain mobilized for war, Bell told the Archbishop of his unsuitability for the post, of his extreme shyness and reserve. Nonetheless, he stayed at Lambeth for three days. Why did he decide to set aside his shyness? Bell had failed to equal the First he achieved in Mods with a similar result in Greats. He was therefore no doubt relieved by the trust the Archbishop placed in him. There was undoubtedly a second and more immediate factor. As so many of his contemporaries were volunteering in response to the King's call – that great unequal sacrifice which occurred before conscription – Bell recognized the need to give way. Accordingly, in December he began his political apprenticeship with Davidson.

This was not any political apprenticeship. The older man, it should be recalled, had been trained for high politics by Archbishop Tait, who was at Lambeth between 1862 and 1882. Bell's apprenticeship occurred at a time when, largely in response to the sheer force of Victorian Christianity, the Church of England stood at an apex of political influence unknown since the reign of Laud. Bell took up his duties with Davidson a little over four months after the declaration of war on Germany. Arriving at Canterbury when the main party was absent, Bell went into the cathedral, which houses the tomb of Thomas à Becket. Bell's own stewardship was to offer no less a challenge to the secular authorities. As with Becket it was based on his Christian faith, although his fidelity to his heavenly Master was possibly more straightforward than that of Becket.

Before taking up residence, Bell had arranged an ecumenical gathering at Lambeth to consider the impact of the Great War. Writing shortly afterwards, Bell prophetically stated that the cause of the Kingdom of God was greater than the cause of the patriot.[7] Even on this score, Bell's ideas were therefore already set before he came to Lambeth. Moreover, his life's greatest test had already been decided intellectually. Only the test of courage awaited him.

The European dimension

Today's ecumenical movement was stirred into existence by the conference staged by missionary societies in Edinburgh at the dawn of the twentieth century. The European dimension to Bell's ecumenical vision began when, in the autumn of 1919, Davidson sent Bell to Holland as part of an Anglican delegation to the first ecumenical gathering following the closure of hostilities. Here Bell met the German delegation. He also met the Swedish primate, Archbishop Söderblom of Uppsala. If Davidson was the journeyman training his pupil in the skills of his trade, it was Söderblom who opened Bell's eyes to the role inspirational leadership can play in the events of humankind. So Bell entered on to the wider international stage, one on which he was to play such an outstanding part.

Davidson had taught Bell one of the most important lessons a master can pass to a pupil – the use of time. This allowed Bell simultaneously to play to a number of distinct audiences during his long stewardship as Bishop of Chichester. There was first his own diocese. Despite all of his other work, here was his primary task. There is everything to support the view, and no evidence to the contrary, that Bell met these duties as conscientiously as any other member of the bench of bishops at the time. Indeed, some of his weaker clergy must have wished Bell had been a little less assiduous in carrying out his responsibilities. But Bell did not believe that the functions of a diocesan were limited by arbitrary geographical boundaries. He was a bishop in the Anglican Communion and his vision paralleled its worldwide base. He also had duties to members of the international Church which, while often located in distinct areas, belonged to the greater community.

This is not the place to debate the nature of the Ecumenical Movement, and whether it amounts to little more than the acceptable face for practising the inward-looking politics of decline. It was nevertheless this Ecumenical Movement and its contacts which drew Bell into the cockpit of twentieth-century politics, namely Germany.

It is in respect of Germany that we see most clearly one of Bell's determining characteristics. He was one of nature's conciliators. An argument had hardly been broached before his pen was at work drafting an acceptable resolution. For most of his life it is impossible to think of George Bell without first considering his natural inclination to bring parties together, and to help them to see how much they agreed with each other. It made of him a trusted figure sitting above any particular faction. Even his beloved Dietrich Bonhoeffer realized that behind those china-like startling blue eyes was a backbone of steel. The metal was, however, not there to give thought to partial affections, but resolutely to work for an agreement. Bell moved easily and naturally as a leader in the Ecumenical Movement. The politics of Life and Work, that half of the Ecumenical Movement led by Bell, centred around Germany and the growing division between the mainstream German Christians and a rebellious minority known as the Confessing or Confessional Church.

Bell did not see this minority in the same way as most British commentators. A common mistake was to interpret what was happening in Germany once the Nazis had seized power as though the events were unfolding in the shire counties.[8] In no way was the Confessing Church's opposition similar to, say, Solidarity's stand against their communist masters. The vast majority of the Confessing pastors were supporters of Hitler but rejected his candidate for *Reichsbischof* (the title adopted in 1933 for the head of the united German Evangelical Church). They believed that the Weimar Republic had been an aberration. The Confessing Church was not a group of dissidents struggling to maintain Western culture in a country overrun by a new barbarism. The new barbarism was already there, and in most respects they supported it. It is significant that while 1,858 pastors were killed at the front, only 21 perished in prison.

It was around the question of perceived truth that the Confessing Church was grouped. It felt itself caught in a struggle against a false theology. Bell, however, saw the issue as one of a fight against evil actions. This division of ideas is most clearly defined in a missive written with typically Germanic force by Dietrich Bonhoeffer to Bell following the latter's Ascensiontide letter. Dietrich questioned Bell's reference to: 'of a loyalty to what they [the pastors] believed to be the Christian truth'. Dietrich pleaded: 'Could you not say perhaps: to what is the Christian truth?' Bell would not give way even to someone who was as close to him as Bonhoeffer.

Bell's unwillingness to close the ecumenical door on the German Christians, or his refusal to give an imprimatur to the Confessing Church's definition of truth, must not blind us to how quickly the then Bishop of Chichester saw into the heart of Nazi ideology. Bell stands out in almost instantaneously realizing the nature of a totalitarian regime, and he saw this so clearly because of his beliefs about the omnipotence of God. Here he was being highly political, but he registered his opposition as that of a cleric. Bell's initiative was controlled by the ease with which he saw the world through God's eyes. By disputing the regime's right to control the thinking and beliefs of the young, Bell cut to the quick of the regime's ambitions for total domination.

Daphne Hampson's research details Bell's influence on the Nazi regime in its early years of power, of his almost instinctive knowledge of how to pitch an appeal so as to catch the Nazis by the tail of their own propaganda. She also gives us a catalogue of his efforts to protect the Confessing Church, as well as the Aryan Christians, while welcoming and seeking ever to extend safety to would-be refugees.[9] Here is a wonderfully effective essay on how the Nazis mistakenly perceived the role of the established Church in British politics and society, and how Bell was able to play this snobbery with the gentlest but most effective of touches.

Consistency or change?

What it is necessary to consider are those aspects of Bell's German initiatives which can be used to suggest that, as Bell became more isolated, the nature of his response changed. In this theatre it is the failure of Bell's strategy to persuade the Allies of the value of driving a wedge between the totalitarian regime and the German people which is most relevant. Certainly the rebuffs Bell suffered here must have added to his sense of isolation. To unravel the various forces at work we have to comprehend that part of Bell's character which cast him in the role of conciliator, even to the point of advocating a negotiated peace, and then to judge whether conciliation was the characteristic which dominated his nature.

Bell not only advocated a negotiated peace, but he did so after Germany started to overrun much of Europe. It is at this point that Bell became divorced from much of the liberal opinion which had upheld and even admired his attempts at negotiating the rapids between British and German politics prior to 1939. But once war looked inevitable – as it did to most people after the Munich euphoria had given way to a more sombre reading of events – public opinion gathered up its courage and determination in preparation for Britain's greatest struggle yet.

For much of the inter-war period Bell's views had fallen well within mainstream political debate. Here the views of the economist J. M. Keynes played a crucial formative role, which he set out in one of the most influential tracts ever written. *The Economic Consequences of the Peace* attacked the Versailles Peace Treaty, which he alleged imposed grotesque penalties on Germany. Germany had in fact proposed a fine, equal to 22.4 per cent of French national income after the 1870 war, which was paid in full in three years.[10] But Keynes' assertions quickly became conventional wisdom among politicians and the wider public, who were ready to explain away or minimize German failure to pay reparations, or to question Germany's subsequent military actions which had been prohibited by the peace treaty.

As middle-ground opinion began to reassess its stance on Germany Bell was left stranded, appearing to believe still in the substance of the spell Keynes had so devilishly cast in the immediate aftermath of World War I. Simultaneously, the process by which Bell was considered unsound by that part of the Establishment gathered pace. Bell was perhaps not to know that proposals for a negotiated peace were generally initiated as a Nazi ploy. Even so, it is not hard to understand the attitude of the War Cabinet and the consequential further hardening of attitudes by Stanley Baldwin's government towards Bell. While such hostility did not deter him, his persistence made it almost inevitable that any message brought back from Stockholm in 1942 would be dismissed. Bell had been sent by the government on a diplomatic mission to help sell the Allied case, and it was during this visit that he had a remarkable meeting with some of the leading German Resistance figures. The message Bell brought home was as simple as it was dramatic. A group was plotting to kill Hitler. Would the British government make public their intention to treat a post-Nazi government differently at any peace negotiations than would be the inevitable response to a beaten Nazi regime? No such statement was forthcoming.

We need to pause to consider what must have gone on in Bell's mind as a result of the government's abject rebuttal of the case he put for the Confessing Church, as well as the wider claims of the resistance movement. Here we need to return to that political apprenticeship which Bell served. Lambeth, at that time, acted as a linchpin and touched all of the parts of the constitution where power was exercised.[11]

Politics, while obviously dominated by the Westminster–Whitehall axis, was nevertheless influenced by the court and the established Church to a degree which is now unimaginable. It was in these three closely inter-related worlds of Parliament, court and the Church, these different parts of what were then the 'effective constitution', to use Bagehot's phrase, that Bell moved as his master's ambassador. But, because of his qualities and the trust which Davidson so obviously placed in him, Bell was no mere cipher. He became a player, and in so doing would have learned the rules by which that most elitist of groups operated. More immediately, his failure to be taken seriously by the Establishment could only increase his sense of being marginalized. It is against this background that we have to consider Bell's public judgements on the propriety of the Allies' war effort. Early involvement here added even further to his sense of being a pariah. His own dean once barred him from preaching in his own cathedral. Just as Bell's abilities allowed him to perceive the full evil of the Nazi regime more quickly than almost any other observer, so too was he led to the great moral question which lay at the heart of an age of total war.

Baldwin's belief that the bomber would always get through had a profound impact on what there was of Britain's defence strategy. If the bomber could make it to these shores, then retaliation was the only possible deterrent. For that Britain required a bombing force. Here, then, was the genesis of a strategy which almost cost Britain the war. Bombers were built at the expense of other types of fighter aircraft. But bombers needed the protection of fighters if they were to stand a reasonable chance of getting near their targets, and those fighters were also needed to defend Britain's airspace. The failure to get the balance right between fighters and bombers had a further consequence other than that of putting at risk the outcome of the entire war effort. It also meant that bombers were the main weapon at our disposal when Hitler appeared to be sweeping all before him. Bombers were the only way of hitting at Hitler, and even if this was done none too effectively, the exercise was believed to raise morale at home.

Bell's stand against obliteration bombing

These were moves watched carefully by Bell. It says much for the freedom of information in war-time Britain that Bell was able to piece together the bombing strategy by reading reports in *The Times*. Before completing his biography of Bell's own biographer, Ronald Jasper, the liturgist Donald Gray found a large shopping basket filled with what appeared to be torn newspaper cuttings. The cuttings were largely from *The Times*, and the basket contained, in addition, correspondence with Liddell Hart, the great war strategist. Bell clearly did not like the picture he was building up of the nature of Britain's bombing campaign in Nazi Germany.

An early skirmish in the House of Bishops showed how unpopular Bell's line would be. Over so much of the 1930s Bell had the support of his primate, Archbishop Cosmo Lang. It is easy now to understand why Lang is out of fashion. If vanity alone was the measurement, the man was in the premier division.[12] Yet he had a wisdom about Germany which many people in public life boasted not to possess. He thought he had persuaded Bell not to raise the night bombing strategy at the fateful meeting of the House of Bishops in June 1941. Bell's first foray into this campaign was quickly overwhelmed. Cyril Garbett, then Bishop of Winchester, shouted Bell down.[13] The next time Bell raised the issue so openly was in the House of Lords. Bell spoke briefly. Lang, now retired as primate, was there in support. If other bishops, including Garbett, were present in the Lords, for this debate they held their peace.

Bell, I am told, was a poor speaker.[14] Some thought this was the reason he never succeeded to the place for which Davidson had trained him. Here then is one of the curious twists of history. The lobby of the House of Commons is filled with statues of statesmen who were most highly regarded at the time Prince Albert and his companions filled the building with works of art by their friends. Few visitors now recognize any of the exhibits, except possibly that of Mr Gladstone. So too with the reputation of parliamentary speakers. Lang was always regarded as one of the great performers, a man who in his youth was thought might one day be prime minister. His speeches now read as what they are: set period pieces. But Bell's great speech rings differently. It is beautifully constructed, and if Archbishop Fisher thought Bell stuffed too many facts into the script, time offers another, more considered judgement.[15]

Bell made the case for limiting the destructiveness of war on civilians at a time when public sensibilities about the impact of war on civilian populations were not what they are today. Even so, part – but only part – of the speech's great strength comes from the very fact that, characteristically, Bell could see that even this issue could no longer be presented in simplistic terminology. In an age when so many moral judgements have to be made in grey areas, Bell struck one of the hardest there was. The bombing strategy pursued by the Allies was morally unacceptable.

Why did Bell offer this great act of prophecy on the moral limits to total war when all his training and experience – reinforced by what appeared to be his dominant characteristic, compromise – would suggest that he would have once again sought a middle way? We can set aside the idea that Bell's exclusion from the very centre of church life – he had not been offered the bishoprics of Durham, London or Winchester in 1938, 1939 and 1942 respectively – had in any way influenced his judgement. Nor do I think it reasonable to argue that the growing isolation of Bell in public debate, and even in ecclesiastical events, could have led to an erratic judgement. Bell simply did not work in this way. Paradoxically, with the lessening of peer group pressure, the isolation, if anything, helped steel him for the task which awaited him.

The rationale for Bell's position is to be found in an article he wrote as the war clouds burst once again over Europe. 'The Church's Function in Wartime'[16] certainly sets out how he believed the Church should perform its duties in such perilous times. It was his adherence to a strategy where the interests of Church and state were not necessarily coterminous which had played a part in the growing division between him and Lang.

There should be no surprise at Bell's stance. Bell had made plain, at the start of his Lambeth apprenticeship, what his reaction would be. I have already cited Bell's observation, soon after taking up his post at Lambeth, that, for Christians, there could be a higher calling than that of patriot. It must have been a belief which strengthened, if not originated, the stance which Davidson took in World War I. It was certainly a cup which could not now be passed. Bell knew what the Establishment response would be. He had been too well schooled in their ways to think otherwise. While he grieved at his continuing exclusion from a more influential position in the Church's hierarchy, it was a grief which was privately borne.[17] Bell's failure to be considered for Canterbury after Temple's early death gave rise to the only occasion when the Church should have thought seriously about disestablishment. Yet, as is shown by the correspondence between Cyril Garbett, who was now Archbishop of York, and Geoffrey Fisher, who was then Bishop of London, the sights of the Church's most senior stewards could not have been cast lower.[18] The impact of that fateful decision on English Christianity is not the question considered here. It is, however, a tragic footnote to it. The issue is rather the relationship between Bell's character, the nature of prophecy and the legitimacy of its role in political activity.

Bell's stand against obliteration bombing has to be seen in a broader context. It was not an aberration or a unique judgement brought about only by the extremities of the hour. The coherence of Bell's stand is to be found in his Christianity. While the practice of his religion was unfussy, his beliefs went to the very core of his existence. Bell believed that humans were fallen creatures and would therefore ever be open to sinful actions. It was one task of Christianity to provide a code of conduct against which actions could be judged and, hopefully, modified. While the expression of sin would change over time, and while such a development would make the application of the natural law more difficult, that judgement had to be made; it was one of the distinguishing marks of Christian civilization. Bell's immediate task in war-time was to apply the doctrine of the just war to the conduct of that war effort.

It is therefore important to distinguish two levels of activity in Bell's public life. Most activities did not clash with the application of the law, whether it was clearly defined canon law, which he had a duty as a bishop to apply, or a higher moral law. But some actions did. On the application of the moral law there was no compromise. In such circumstances Bell never sought a middle way. He had consistently and firmly applied canon law to those practising excessive liturgical zeal and high-church frippery in his diocese. The judgement on the obliteration bombing was of the same nature. It was merely that the judgement was made on a world stage rather than at parish level. So I challenge the view that, by the late 1930s, Bell had become more radical.[19] It was rather that the events to which Bell applied such steadfastness were themselves radically changed. At any time from 1914 onwards Bell would have made a similar judgement on international affairs. The timing of that judgement was not in his hands.

While the moral law always acted as a framework within which Bell operated, for most of the time its limiting of activities was unremarkable. What was much more apparent was Bell's exercise of Christian charity, of seeing the other person's point of view, and of trying to build on that to achieve agreement. It is therefore a mistake to see Bell's application of principle as somehow a reshaping of his personality. It is merely a question of the hour as to which side of Bell's character would be seen to be the more dominant.

Nor is it true to say that, in applying the moral law, Bell assumed the role of meddling prelate, as that role has been traditionally defined. Bell's incarnational theology stood in stark contrast to that presented by the German Church, for example. Their crude division of God on the one hand, the world on the other, was utterly foreign to Bell's thinking. All that happened in God's domain was of importance. But in the world of day-to-day activities the priest needed to act as a priest, attempting to apply the moral law to human conduct. Poverty, for example, was not simply unfair because, in a Rawlsian sense, an individual, not knowing whether he or she might turn out to be poor, would judge such circumstances unacceptable.[20] It was evil because it mocked part of the creation, and that which was made in God's own image. That was the philosophy Bell began to fashion in his theology combined with his work as an assistant curate at Leeds parish church at the turn of the century. This remained characteristic of Bell's approach to politics, which was always a genuine attempt to see the world through God's eyes. Bell may have been right or wrong on the issues in question. That is not the point. What he could not be fairly accused of was of being a priest using secular political arguments and advancing them under the guard of his clerical collar.

It is doubtful whether Bell saw his heroic stand against obliteration bombing as an act of prophecy. For him it was simply the right action at the right time. Such a judgement again stressed the coherence of Bell's behaviour and the way he saw himself operating in the political arena. Two patterns of behaviour are clearly discernible. For most of the time, Bell was involved in practical activities. Intervening in human affairs amounted to much more than the occasional foray into the public domain. Sometimes, for example, it was necessary to call attention to the plight of the refugees. But most of the time was spent attending to their individual needs. Indeed, it was from such primary work that Bell gained so much of the ammunition to make special his public comments. Bell's politics were a true blend of both principle and practicality.

The way Bell saw public figures influencing the course of a political debate ran in parallel to this approach. For most of the time, circumstances determined that Christians would be most effective in a role similar to that which yeast plays in cooking, losing its identity but in the process creating something new. Other times called for Christians to bear witness, as a light on the hill. The hour called for action which taught a message above the hurly-burly of everyday activity. Bell's life flowers with examples of both kinds of political approaches which are set out in the New Testament. Acting as a light on the hill might be, to us, acts of prophecy, but I would suggest such a categorization would merely call forth a puzzled expression from Bell. To him it was one form of political activity, and its need was governed by circumstances rather than any textbook commendation on correct political action.

To separate the politics of the 1930s, and suggest that those dramatic events illustrate a development in Bell's beliefs, or in his response, is mistaken. I now see more clearly what Mrs Temple meant by the reported response of her husband to a typical piece of Bell behaviour. The bishops would believe that a debate had been settled, only for those china-blue eyes of George Bell to pop open and for the discussion to begin all over again.

It is the wholesomeness and total consistency of George Bell which is so attractive. It is no surprise, as those with memories of prelates like Temple, whose appeal was in part the force of their personalities, take their leave, that the significance of George Bell becomes ever more easy to recognize. Indeed, as the twentieth century recedes, the importance of George Bell to that century becomes ever more apparent.

7

Piety and Provocation: A study of George Bell[1]

What are we to make of George Bell? He is remembered largely for his stance against the Allied obliteration bombing of Germany in World War II, which some suggest cost him the succession to the archbishopric of Canterbury. This event is invariably presented as a period piece, highlighting what was once the Church's influence in the life of the nation, and in particular at its most critical time. Bell studies have inevitably looked back in time.

But, as Andrew Chandler makes plain in his new study, there is much more to Bell than this anti-bombing stance, important though it undoubtedly is. Here, in Chandler's portrait, we find Bell raised above what has been, until now, a limited debate to reposition him in relation to an agenda which is very much one set in our own time.

A new perspective

No one is better placed than Chandler to represent Bell to what is in so many crucial respects a very different world to the one in which Bell worked and which he tried to change. Chandler brutally side-steps the usual timid hero-worship accorded to Bell, but his reasons for doing so are intriguing. Chandler observes that Bell 'is undoubtedly a peripheral figure in the history of the twentieth century as we are coming to read it in the words of historians'. Our sight of Bell is diminished because of the way historians train us to view events and how that training has ordered what we now see as important, let alone heroic events. In contrast, and as a result of Chandler's work, we now have a study that frees Bell from the fads of historians.

Chandler's aim is to place Bell at the centre of 'a far greater narrative' than his attack on the Allied war strategy alone. Much of the country's efforts after World War I were to try to return to what was seen as the golden Edwardian age which had been rudely and unnecessarily interrupted by what is cruelly called the Great War. What we are implicitly being invited to accept here in Chandler's analysis is a world in which the growing chaos and horror that is so firmly linked to Nazism is not, however tragically, an aberration in a record of what would otherwise be viewed as unimpeded progress. Nazism Chandler sees not as an end but, rather, as a prelude to today's horrors. And, therefore, for those people who are so often offered only alienation, dispossession and destruction, Bell has a far greater narrative role in standing by and talking alongside those 'who yearn to speak new and bold words to a world in disarray'.

So here we find the outline of a portrait of what Bell sees as the verities of Christian civilization and of him bravely speaking of these to a world which was much excited by its own destruction. Here is an extraordinary paradox: Bell, if anyone, was groomed for the top ecclesiastical job and had the prophetic vision that would have enabled him to fill that office with great distinction. Yet that prophetic role ensured he would tell awkward truths to those who did not wish to hear them. The consequences for Bell, in terms of earthly rewards, require no comment.

Chandler reveals his own great strength as an historian by delicately illustrating the interplay between social and political forces. Bell's admittance to Westminster School is viewed as a preparation for the world of authority. That role was affirmed when he later gained a place in the heart of the orderly and privileged world at Christ Church, Oxford. There then followed a decade of apprenticeship as the Archbishop of Canterbury's chaplain and key member of staff.

The international contacts Bell made at Canterbury were strengthened and extended during his short tenure as Dean of Canterbury. He not only opened up the cathedral to visitors (too many cathedrals at the time were operating as private clubs) but began reintroducing art and drama as a means of relaying great truths about our existence.

In his magisterial study on the post-war Church Commissioners,[2] Chandler repositions the role of Archbishop Fisher, who was appointed Archbishop of Canterbury over Bell. In this much shorter study, Chandler shows what a great ally Archbishop Lang was to Bell in the period leading up to and into war and compares this relationship sharply with the negative, not to say hostile, response to him from William Temple.

At the heart of Chandler's narrative is a belief that Bell was right to pursue peace, even in times of war, as the peace would be less destructive than the consequences of total war. It is an argument we do not hear much about now, but it has an eerie relevance to the current debate on our involvement in the wars in those stricken territories that were once seen as the cradle of civilization. I don't accept Chandler's line, but there are few historians who could deploy this argument to better effect. In doing so, Chandler provides a totally new perspective to George Bell's greatness.

8

Two heroes, one message

Let me say something more about my hero George Bell, and consider him alongside Conrad Noel, another person who unexpectedly became one of my heroes. George Kennedy Allen Bell was a priest. There is, I believe, no higher calling. Surprisingly for a modern priest, he had a major cultural impact on this country. The revival of religious drama owes a great deal to his efforts. It was he, for example, who suggested to T. S. Eliot that he write the play which became *Murder in the Cathedral*. This particular turbulent priest trained as chaplain to Archbishop Davidson. Davidson, in turn, had been chaplain to Archbishop Tait. There was therefore a form of apostolic succession, whereby one generation prepared the next generation's primate and, in the case of Frederick Temple, sired him!

I was not immediately attracted to Noel whereas Bell filled me with admiration and joy that such beings can exist. I therefore believed that the differences between the two would be so marked that an obvious structure would emerge for what I wish to add here.

The differences

There are differences which clearly ought to be marked. There are differences in their political abilities and in their political skills. But, perversely, I am now not so sure that the differences are of importance when compared to the similarities. In learning a little of Noel and in reflecting further on Bell, I was afforded a further insight into the nature of idealism, vision, prophecy, or however you wish to describe what motivated both men, and their relevance to politics. However, let me begin with what I see as the clear differences between these two great characters.

They are three in all. As we are addressing the distinctions between two Englishmen, the first is, inevitably, a class difference.

Noel was clearly upper-class, a grandson of the Earl of Gainsborough. And that background was evident in the manner in which he projected his views. It was manifest in a confidence, which sometimes could be more accurately described as arrogance, as he went about his daily round. There is also more than a hint of 'slumming' about some of Noel's activities and, because of his background, he emanated a particular attraction for those working-class people for whom the aristocrats still held some particular and unique appeal. And yet when all those vast advantages of class are recorded, it is essential to recall that he was also a truly charismatic character, enormously skilled, and a music-hall artist of the first order.

Bell, in contrast, was stubbornly middle-class. His father was vicar of Wimbledon, in those days no minor living, who subsequently became a canon of Canterbury. So we cannot view Bell's life as one of particular hardship. But his life and background did personify solid middle-class virtues. He believed in getting on with the job and had a distaste, almost a horror, of show; he displayed a total lack of egotism – not, I think, a charge that one could easily level at Conrad Noel. And yet, while Bell was the sort of person you would want, in Tawney's phrase, to have beside you in the trench as you go over the top to face the Hun, he was not someone you would probably want to meet in the pub. He certainly would not be a member of the local darts team and would be an uneasy neighbour in the next hospital bed.

So much for class differences. There were also character differences. Noel's aristocratic temperament stunted his democratic convictions. He was frequently unable or unwilling to appreciate the unacceptable contradictions inherent in some of his positions. Indeed, those contradictions on more than one occasion made him look foolish. His call for the furtherance of Catholic order, for example, was matched only by his own disobedience to that order. Catholic order was, therefore, for other people, not for Conrad. His fanaticism led him to be both unkind and intolerant in a way which seems sometimes to have given him pleasure. Let me give one example. Noel's bishop for much of his time at Thaxted was John Watts-Ditchfield, who criticized Noel's decision to celebrate the feast of the Assumption. The Bishop invited Noel to lunch in order to discuss the matter. Noel refused this offer of a meal, stating that he could not dine at the table of a heretic. Quite how Noel believed he had the authority to denounce his bishop and to pronounce judgement on heresy remains a mystery. More significantly, Noel failed to appreciate the irony of holding such extreme views while simultaneously asserting the central importance of Catholic order. Bell could not have been more different. His diffidence, and his total lack of self, stands in marked contrast to Noel's near arrogance.

The final difference that I wish to stress is their approach to politics. Noel's political philosophy was backward-looking. He was obsessed by a supposed medieval hegemony. He emphasized an imaginary rural past. He said very little about how to help shape the future, although he was an avid critic of current practice.

The result of Conrad Noel's obsession with a medieval past and a Catholic order was a blinkered vision of any way forward which led him to make the most extraordinary judgements. For Noel, the damnable Soviet collective farm system was at first seen as a re-establishment of a manorial system. The millions who died in the forced labour camps might have told him a different story. Moreover, if we are in the business of comparisons, how would the medieval serf rate his experience against his equivalent in the communist collective system?

Bell, in contrast, was hardnosed in his approach to politics and to its daily business. We have to recall his experience as chaplain to Archbishop Davidson, and the fact that the Archbishop of Canterbury, ex officio, then played a role in politics which no archbishop plays or could play today. The archbishop was then the linchpin between Parliament, the court and Whitehall. And Bell, as Davidson's trusted advisor, helper and soulmate in this activity, had a training which few others received. This solid grounding in how the Establishment thought and operated meant that Bell cannot have been greatly surprised by the reaction of that ultra-conservative body to his stand on obliteration bombing.

This was to have been the substance of the distinction which I wanted to underline between these two men: concise, crisp and clear. However, the similarities which, however reluctantly, I have discerned between these two great characters swamp any differences that I can put forward. There are, in fact, seven similarities on which I would like to dwell.

The similarities

To our disadvantage, both men have been inadequately captured by the historian's lens. Bell's biography was to have been written by Norman Sykes, the Dean of Winchester, the foremost ecclesiastical historian of the century. Sykes would have produced a life which matched the great book that Bell himself wrote of his own mentor, Davidson. There is a mischievous story, which was told to me by Canon Roy Porter, one-time chaplain to Bell, that when Sykes died, Hatty, Bell's wife, became anxious for the life to be completed before she herself died. She had heard from Archbishop Fisher that a man called Jasper wrote books, and particularly books on 'the religious'. Jasper was indeed a greatly talented historian: his book on Headlam, now a forgotten bishop, is a fine piece of work. And yet when Jasper was asked to write Bell's life, his interests were developing, becoming heavily concentrated on changes in liturgical forms of worship. Above all, Jasper was driven by the need to finish the life before Hatty died. The result is that Bell has had imposed upon him a hurriedly completed death mask which now distorts the way we see the true man in all his magnificence.

Conrad Noel has been even worse served than Bell. Towards the end of his life he wrote a very short autobiography. I began reading that book but I could not finish it. It was poorly written and clearly the work of an old man nearing the end of his days. It is a totally inaccurate record of this man's remarkable gifts and gives no hint whatsoever of Conrad Noel's greatness. Despite the subsequent publications by people like Ken Leech, Robert Woodifield and Gareth Turner, there is no significant life of Conrad Noel. He and Bell represent two great lacunae in twentieth-century British ecclesiastical biography.

Another, and unarguably more important, similarity is that both were men of God. Each tried to see the world through God's eyes, and the only difference here is one of emphasis, being derived from their contrasting characters. Noel, I believe, because he was more sensual, more extrovert, more flamboyant and suffered little, if any, reserve, could in one sense portray a fuller and rounder vision of God's presence in this world. Bell's approach, grounded in his character, was also shaped by doctrine and a degree of reserve, to the extent that he made some of the Tractarian high command seem positively loose-living and liberal. Bell had an unusually strong appeal, though, for those Christians whose character led them in his particular direction.

But the view that both men had of God and the world bonded them as sacramentalists. They saw God's glory all around them, and that ubiquitous glory was to be worshipped. God was to be celebrated through that daily round. For those in priestly orders, the saying of the daily offices will be a familiar part of everyday routine. Within this, the psalms and canticles have a major role. The Benedicite, for example, refers to all of the

Lord's works blessing him, the angels of the Lord blessing him, the heavens blessing him, the waters above the firmament blessing him, the powers of the Lord blessing him, the sun and the moon blessing him, and so on for many a long paragraph.

Both Noel and Bell genuinely believed, in the truly Christian sense, in that pantheism whereby the wonders of creation are the proof of God's existence. Both attacked, but Noel to a greater degree, a hatred of those pieties that so restrict our vision of the eternal. The mass, Conrad Noel emphasized, was to be beautiful because it hints at God's beauty. To both Noel and Bell, Jesus is not imprisoned in the blessed sacrament. The blessed sacrament is rather the window on to the world through which we see the universe in its true form. Churches, which ought to be unlocked, are the gateways to paradise.

Any difference in emphasis here again derives from character. Noel was a very physical man. Marriage for him was the most fleshly of sacraments. Not only did it give immediate gratification, but it also demonstrated a physical and intellectual union which hints at the nature of our union with God. To suggest to Bell that marriage was a fleshly sacrament would have made the poor old bishop tense with embarrassment. There was, however, no difference in the sacramental view of the priestly role. Both believed the priest had a very special role to sanctify a place, whether that place was a diocese or a parish. Both served out their stewardship for a long period of time in one place.

Both Bell and Noel had a sense of the position of the English Church and its place in our history. They both instinctively felt that the English nation was made by the English Church. They both knew in their bones that the English Church has helped to form and shape the English character. Both of them were Catholic; neither was Roman. Both of them were the disciples of Percy Dearmer, who did so much to restore a dignified sense of Catholic liturgy in the Church of England, although again Bell was less enthused by the minutiae of the liturgy – he could never, for example, wear his cope properly. All the photographs

I have seen of him show the cope lurching off to one side, and this never seemed to worry him, even when a photograph was about to be taken.

The further similarity between these two great figures was that both were paradoxically beneficiaries of the Establishment. Bell was, as a bishop, the more obvious beneficiary of Establishment patronage. He effectively had the easier time following a traditional career path, going first to Christ Church and then becoming Davidson's chaplain. He was appointed Dean of Canterbury and subsequently Bishop of Chichester.

Noel, on the other hand, because of his views, was unemployed and gradually became nearly unemployable. But, thanks to the patronage of the Countess of Warwick, he came to Thaxted. Without this peculiarly English system of patronage Noel would probably never have had such a living in his stewardship. And yet while both men were, in different ways, beneficiaries of the Establishment, both were prevented by that very same Establishment from playing their full part, and their full worth was never fully recognized or acted upon. Noel's passage was blocked because the hierarchy failed to perceive his greatness. Noel's greatness, in fact, was stunted by the vision others held of his being a stereotyped 'red' priest. Bell's career was stalled because that same hierarchy comprehended only too well the danger that he posed. Here was a man who was prepared, almost single-handedly, to condemn those obliterating bombing raids on Nazi Germany – bombing raids which, I have to confess, I would have supported had I had a voice at the time.

There is yet another similarity. Neither was an original thinker, either politically or theologically. Original thinkers are, and have always been, the very great exception. Yet both Bell and Noel made unique contributions to politics and to theology. Bell, for example, was one of the first in this country to realize that English and European politics would be dominated by Germany during the twentieth century. And Bell, because he had a view about the nature of the Church resembling the body of Christ, was obsessed by Christian unity. Noel, for his part, grafted a Tractarian theology on to political beliefs in a way no other person has managed to do in this country. And in so doing he helped to create that curious but wonderful and genuinely uplifting Christian Socialist tradition in Britain.

To the next similarity: both believed that spiritual redemption is inseparable from material redemption of the poor. But poverty should be abolished because it is evil, not because it hinders salvation. We have only to consider European history, particularly the Middle Ages so beloved of Noel, to see the truth here. Africa today is similarly a testament to the fact that appalling physical conditions are not an insuperable bar to the outward and visible signs of salvation and the leading of holy lives. Bell, it is true to say, was less of a heretic than Noel in this respect, but they both shared the conventional thinking of their time. There is a great case to be made against poverty, but this is not part of it.

The truth, in fact, is the opposite of what they held to be true. It is riches, not poverty, which are the barrier to salvation. It is the greed that comes from riches which prevents the rich from recognizing God on the last dreadful Day of Judgement. For some, their greed will be so great that they will not be able to recognize him. If we were a little more certain about paradise we would be a lot more forceful about the need to liberate the rich. We would be more insistent on the inherent dangers to them of their wealth. We would be more creative in our view that paradise should not be allowed to become a one-class state for the poor.

My final similarity: both Bell and Noel had an eschatological view of the world. It was, of course, given different prominence by both. Their characters made this inevitable. For Bell the great eschatological truth lay like sediment on the river bed over which all the water, all his thinking, all his actions, ran. Noel's eschatological views were constantly erupting like a volcano, with all the excitement, the splendour and the dangers that volcanoes can bring. Yet they both saw the coming of the Kingdom as entailing judgement, and in this sense the Second Coming gave their work a sense of both direction and urgency which is sometimes lacking in today's daily round.

Two heroes

Let me present, if I may, my conclusions about the lives of these two extraordinary and exceptional people.

The first is that both are truly saints, offering us inspiration as we attempt, both collectively and individually, our own passage through life.

Second, both of them are role models for a courageous life. Noel was fearless in his attempt to awaken the whole Church to the true extent of an oppression and evil which he recognized. And he did so knowing, as a consequence, that there would be no preferment from this parish. Similarly, Bell, in attempting to define the limits of physical conflict in an age which had already unleashed total war, knew what the penalties would be for such a stand. He can have been in no doubt that his office, once used in public protest, would ring the end of his chance of succession to the throne of St Augustine at Canterbury. It would count for nothing that he was uniquely qualified and trained for the role. It would matter not at all that he stood head and shoulders above any other potential candidate. Both men must have believed, at least for most of the time, that their courage would end any chance of further advance.

And last, both of them knew that without vision we all perish. Neither was beguiled by that Marxist doctrine that sees forces greater than ourselves governing our destiny. Both believed that ideas, courage, the obligation on the individual to exercise his or her free will, and the all-embracing love of God are the great driving forces in world history. And who are we to disagree?

A final comment about both people. These great figures who have gone before us shared a view about the Kingdom of God and its advance being dependent upon our frail bodies. That is not a secular argument that somehow humankind, by itself, can actually save the world. It is rather a belief that in the Incarnation there was a true emptying out of the Godhead into us. Did God himself at that point limit his powers over us and give us merely the powers of God of knowing good and evil, as Genesis tells us? No. He did far more than that. He gave us a free will of the kind that might appeal to today's rationalists. But if we are free agents in this total sense of God surrendering his sovereignty to us, then it totally reorders the place and the urgency of the Church as our place of worship and of the sacraments as a means of grace.

Here is a final paradox. Part of the genius of the Church of England has been that it has understood how much religion the English will take – which is not very much. That we cannot take much religion has always been understood by the English Church, which intuitively caters for these minimal requirements. But there is nevertheless within that Church a sacramental view about the means of grace. And that Church reorders our emphasis on all that is hauntingly beautiful, not just in church but in everything. And it does this, not because of a wish to develop an aesthetic taste, but rather because it is through our frail bodies that we are messengers of that Kingdom, and these frail bodies are nurtured by that worldly beauty which gives us but a faintest glimpse of God's face. Through beauty we become aware of his presence and we gain some hint of his character. We are thereby strengthened to hold to our true mission, as did Conrad Noel and as did George Bell, of keeping the rumour of God alive in our hearts and in our neighbourhood, in our country and thereby in our world.

Part 3

MADAM INVINCIBLE

Introduction

I love Eleanor Rathbone not simply for her vulnerability, although vulnerable she was. Nor does my heart warm to her because of her choice of goals or the steadfast way she went about pursuing them. Of course this makes her attractive. But the greatest aspect of her attractiveness lies in her willingness rarely, if ever, to compromise and to show that such an approach can be effective politically.

It is the manner in which Eleanor used her talents to the full to become one of our truly great social reformers that leaves me breathless. It is the sheer professionalism she brought to her craft that so impresses. Eleanor did not simply engage with her subject-matter as a lobbyist and MP to change the political position of women and children. She intellectually led the field and so helped the electorate see the world through different eyes. Without an achievement on this scale her legislative goals might not have been reached.

I also so admire her for the range of issues she mastered and to which she contributed in Parliament. The record speaks for itself. Day after day she was on her feet making ministers defend their actions. No wonder the university graduates who returned her to Parliament did so each time with larger and larger majorities. She effectively set an example of how elected representatives should behave in the public domain.

Had she not been a woman, and had she compromised her independence and become a party figure, she would be remembered for the greatness that was hers. What kind of country is it that wipes from its memory someone who happens to be a woman, and who cocks a snook at a system in an age where party was becoming ever more important in allowing access to power and influence?

9

Citizenship and the politics of behaviour: lessons from Eleanor Rathbone's thought

―――•◦•―――

Almost no one I know can recall who Eleanor Rathbone was. Yet I regard her as one of the most impressive backbench Members of Parliament ever.[1] It is true that her name is not linked in the public mind with a single great event, unlike another of those outstanding backbench Members of Parliament, William Wilberforce – in his case with the abolition of slavery in the British Empire. Nor does her work have the immediate pull of Lord Shaftesbury's campaign for the Factory Acts; Shaftesbury illustrates how humanitarianism surmounted laissez-faire-ism when this doctrine was supposedly carrying all before it. Nor, somehow, is Eleanor's work associated with her name, in the way Cobden and Bright are linked with the campaigning that they undertook to abolish the Corn Laws; their work established Britain as a free trade nation in food as well as manufacture.

History has been written in such a way that the contribution made by this extraordinary individual, who happened to be a woman, has been largely ignored and forgotten. Her Family Allowance Act, for that is how the House of Commons attributed the coalition government's measure, has had as significant and enduring an impact on the lives of children as did Shaftesbury's great Factory Acts. Part of her 'trouble', though she would not have used such a word, was that Eleanor was not associated simply with a single reform, although the introduction of family allowances undoubtedly caused a significant change in the balance of power within families. She led a series of successful campaigns, but many of them were to change attitudes, to sound warnings and to rectify particular injustices in what were then too often described as 'far-away countries' and therefore, in a sense, off-stage. Yet, as Eleanor's record of firsts is truly remarkable, let me recall a number of different aspects of her greatness.

Eleanor ranks among the major feminist influences in gaining the parliamentary vote for women. At the same time she takes feminism into its second phase when it is clear that the franchise reforms of 1918 had failed to protect the position working-class women had won for themselves and their families during the Great War.

Although Eleanor was always a feminist she was not limited by her feminism. Along with Churchill, Eleanor was among the first to recognize the enormity of Hitler's potential for evil. Not surprisingly, perhaps, she was one of the clearest advocates for rearmament when the nation's heart governed its head in terms of the growing Nazi threat. After failing to persuade the Allies to make the saving of the Jews a war aim, Eleanor nevertheless directly helped countless Jews to escape the gas chambers.

Eleanor was not fooled, as many were, and saw early on the evils of Stalin, predicting that he would strike a deal with his totalitarian soulmate in Germany. She was politically fearless on numerous war-time issues, such as opposing the coalition government's returning to certain death in the USSR those Polish officers who had fought so bravely to keep Britain free. It is to our eternal shame that these brave souls were sent back to their deaths. While Eleanor holds the distinction of being among the first to campaign for military action against Germany, she was, likewise, part of a very small band demanding the adequate feeding of a beaten German nation, in part from

British supplies, at a time when Britain's own living standards had been screwed down almost to breaking point. And yet Eleanor still found time to achieve more than any other single campaigner to advance the position of women in countries ruled by the British Colonial Office.

And so the list continues.

Why should an outstanding individual such as Eleanor have disappeared beneath the waves of public consciousness? Part of the answer centres on our failure as a nation adequately to teach the next generation about our past. Here, however, I wish to look to the future by illustrating Eleanor's continuing relevance for today's agenda. There are two areas of her political thinking, on citizenship and on motherhood, and the particular way these two issues should combine in our minds, that are again highly relevant to our current debate.

An exercise that brings citizenship back into the equation might have surprised and dismayed Eleanor in equal measure. At the point when Eleanor died she could have been forgiven for thinking that the issue of citizenship had been settled, as far as any political issue can be decided. A proper recognition of motherhood, she would have accepted, was still a goal to be achieved. Eleanor knew more than most observers that citizenship was not simply about getting the vote. Though an undeniably significant achievement, the vote was not an end in itself but rather a means to the end of a self-governing commonwealth. Through the vote, citizens could shape society's arrangements so that each of them could achieve their best selves. But in gaining that self-governing commonwealth, motherhood had a pivotal role to play.

Let me begin by setting out how I view the establishment of citizenship in this country and, equally importantly, the political ideas which, by winning almost universal assent, made citizenship in this form a way of life for this country. I also wish to stress how Eleanor's views, which developed beyond the goal of an equal franchise, have an extraordinary relevance to today's debate. I will then go on to suggest why the seemingly inexorable rise of today's yobbish culture strikes at the very foundations of this peaceable kingdom, which was the overall aim of most of the campaigners for franchise reform. A peaceful kingdom was the end product of a set of political ideas on citizenship which the British had taken to their hearts.

The citizenship journey

I turn quickly to the first of these themes – the model which best explains to me how citizenship was established in our country. Citizenship in Britain did not arrive by means of revolution, as it did in other countries. Its establishment here was a gradual process, and that process I can best liken to that of a train journey, as the franchise was gradually extended to greater numbers of people.

This train journey towards full citizenship begins with the train leaving its starting point with only a few passengers on board. As the journey progresses, the train stops at a number of stations where would-be passengers anxiously wait to join the journey towards full citizenship. The entry ticket for this journey is a personal one. Passengers are allowed on board once they have shown the male elite that the type of person they are is consistent with the status which the vote bestows. The waiting travellers know and accept these terms, so much so that, as the train approaches its destination, the whole adult population is safely and willingly on board.

This is the unspoken model of citizenship that Eleanor and practically all her contemporaries held in their mind's eye. It was an analogy which held true during the whole period of Eleanor's long and active life and continued for some time after her death in 1946 – indeed, the run-up to a situation which, as well as those early post-war years, now turns out to be unique. Some of us were fortunate enough to experience what it was like to live in a peaceful, self-governing commonwealth. Returning

117

to this ideal state of civil government will require a fundamental change in British politics. We will need to become as obsessed by a person's behaviour as we were once by class.

The growth of British citizenship assumed that the urge in each of us to achieve our best selves, and thereby become full citizens, would become and remain universal. This most basic assumption underpinning British citizenship is being fundamentally challenged. The challenge was at first so insignificant that it was easily dismissed. The challenge now to what British citizenship entails, and the way of life with which it is intimately bound up, is widespread and serious, and the threat to it is growing.

Let me revert to the train analogy to illustrate these more recent events. The train, as it approaches its pick-up points, still finds many of the awaiting company wishing to board. Many new arrivals to this country, for example, are only too anxious to join this great journey. It is true that, once on board, some of these new arrivals complain that they experience a somewhat frosty reception from passengers already there. Even so, the wish of much of this section of the community is to get on to the train.

Open revolt

That wish is no longer universal among some of the host community who, while collecting at the railway stations, have no intention of joining the great British citizenship journey. Worse still, they don't understand the point of the train journey, even though tradition is still strong enough to pull them towards their nearest station. Some of this mob hang around in aggressive mood. A growing proportion of what is overall an overwhelmingly poor white group – but is, of course, of a different composition in the areas where there has been large-scale immigration from the Indian sub-continent – do not limit their disagreement to a refusal to buy a train ticket. This group also expresses a direct hostility to those who have bought their ticket and are waiting on the platform. This hostile mass often displays a loathing of those who are already on board. Actual and would-be passengers know that the train journey is now no longer the trouble-free and peaceful event it once was.

The task is not simply one of restoring order at the station, although that is the far from unreasonable demand of actual and would-be passengers. There is a need to set out once again what is the basis of British citizenship and why, if anyone wishes to draw upon its advantages, they likewise need to buy an entry ticket. What that entry ticket entails takes me to my second theme. Or, to put it another way, what was the genesis of the ideas that made being a decent citizen so accepted that no one, until recently, questioned the nature of the magic that delivered a self-governing peaceable kingdom?

It is important to remind ourselves just how recent is this attack on our peaceable kingdom. Coming to this country as a refugee after living in many other European countries, Geoffrey Elton paid this tribute in his inaugural lecture as Regis Professor of History at Cambridge. Let me stress that Elton's observations were made as recently as 1984. Elton commented:

> I know very well that [this country] is not a realm of unfailing virtue and goodness. That does not alter the fact that it managed to produce a form of existence which is freer of sins against one's neighbour than any other community has attained…it excels in having come to terms with the fact that people in large numbers need both to be conscious of one another and leave one another alone.[2]

Making a peaceable kingdom

What was the basis of this peaceable kingdom that so brilliantly developed a form of urban life which respected the space individuals need around them if they are not to suffocate? There were three beliefs which came into play, each reinforcing the others, and each helped to build the peaceable kingdom Geoffrey Elton described as existing less than 25 years ago. These beliefs are:

- the belief in respectability
- the belief in character
- the belief in our best selves.

First, let me touch upon the urge for respectability, which is still such a force for good in our society. Its roots are to be found in the latter stages of the Evangelical Revival, when the faith preached by the Revival's leadership began to be lived out naturally in the lives of ordinary families.[3] We cannot properly comprehend the type of Britain in which we grew up without considering the impact of this great Revival, starting, some would say, in the eighteenth century and sweeping much before it in the following century. The records of the nineteenth century testify to its effect. When we step into the pages of, say, *Lark Rise to Candleford*, we meet those desperately poor, humble but unbelievably decent farm labourers who believed that they had a personal relationship with their Maker, and that they were responsible to that God for each and every one of their actions. Abiding by local codes of behaviour, combined with a sense of direct responsibility for one's actions, was important in shaping the kind of person the British aspired to be.

Respectability was closely intertwined with the idea of moral character. The concept of character is now all too often demeaned by presenting it as a means of class control whereby the middle and upper classes pass judgement on those 'below' them. This is not how the idea of character was then perceived. The great radical forces of late Victorian and Edwardian society were constantly seeking means to promote public virtue. As Jose Harris notes, character was not a moral means-test by another name.[4] Moral character and active citizenship were the building blocks of a well-ordered and virtuous state.

It was because of the character and respectability of so much of the burgeoning labour movement that the vote was conceded.

Even the most ardent critics had to concede that trade unions, mutual aid societies and friendly societies, the constituent parts of the labour movement, were in fact mini democracies. Awarding the vote was merely a public recognition that citizenship had already been achieved.

When Eleanor went up to Oxford in 1893 she read Greats, a course then taught through the lens carefully ground by the English Idealist T. H. Green. I have attempted to set out in the introductory chapter the importance of this single academic, seeing his success as shaping ideas which became, in effect, a public ideology in this country.[5] For Green, and for his followers like Eleanor, political citizenship was not the end of the process but its beginning. By service to our fellow men and women, starting within the family and radiating outwards, each of us would be able to achieve our best selves, which guaranteed a basic social citizenship. This objective, of achieving our best selves, was to English Idealists the main purpose of life and, as English Idealism forged a new public ideology, this was the goal to which practically the whole population subscribed.

Limits of voting power

Eleanor's role in ensuring the franchise was extended to women is well recorded. Her Idealist view, that achieving the vote was merely the beginning of a journey of developing our best selves, was rudely ruptured almost as soon as the ballot boxes were opened in 1918. This was the first election in which women, providing they were over 30, gained the vote on the same basis as it had been awarded to males aged 21 and over.

Eleanor was quick to notice from her observations in her home city of Liverpool that the vote gained by working-class women did little to protect the economic positions they had gained for themselves during the war years. The promise the coalition government had made to trade union leaders to restore the status quo in the workplace once the Armistice was signed was rigorously enforced. Losing their jobs to the returning soldiers was not the only injury inflicted upon working-class women. The separation allowances paid to them while their husbands were away fighting were similarly stripped away by the hard-faced men who had made money out of the war, as the membership of the 1918 House of Commons has been described.

In striking out on a new agenda, Eleanor tried to maintain good relations with the first wave of feminists who had a single objective of individual women fulfilling their full potentiality. It was the novelist Winifred Holtby, Vera Brittain's great friend, who declared she was an old feminist 'because she disliked all that feminism implied and wanted an end to the whole business so that she could get on with her own work'.[6] Eleanor saw the goal differently. Her objective was that women as a group should fulfil their talents. Making this objective practical politics led Eleanor beyond the vote and into new territory. She was quick to appreciate that it was inadequate for feminists always to shadow the male agenda. Equality shaped on these terms would necessarily be constrained by a world seen only through men's eyes.

Endowing motherhood

The starting point for the new feminist agenda had to be what women needed to fulfil the potentialities of their own natures. Eleanor's co-worker, Eva Hubback,[7] was even more unforgiving to those who saw the aim of feminism as merely getting women to the top of a man's world, although she was not against that goal. Eva insisted that women had different needs and possessed a different outlook from men, and that these differences must prevail in their most important group occupation, which is that of maternity. Many of the new feminists, such as Eleanor and Eva, did not view maternity itself as a disability, as did many feminists. They argued, I believe rightly, that maternity was only a disability because of the low status society accorded to women, and particularly to women with children.

Motherhood was not only important on these terms. It was equally important in that it formed the crucible within which the idea of respectability, of developing character and achieving our best selves, was alloyed into a new generation of citizens. For it was within the family that the social side of human nature was nurtured.

It is worth again citing William Temple, the one-time Archbishop of Canterbury, who defined original sin in the following terms. Each of us, when we first open our eyes, sees the world as though we are at its centre. Well-functioning families begin with this starting point, but then go on to help us accept that there are possibly three, four or more other people living in the same household who similarly view themselves as the centre of the world. Peaceful co-existence requires careful and continual negotiations between each household member so that the integrity of each is preserved and enhanced in a manner which similarly values each other member, although in successful families most members are rarely aware that these negotiations are nearly continuous. Such successful negotiations equip each of us with the social skills necessary to negotiate the outside world.

Family failure

If there is a single root cause of the rise and rise of yobbish and anti-social behaviour, it is that an increasing number of families are failing to impart these social skills to their offspring, and are thereby undermining the kind of universal citizenship which, until so very recently, we took for granted. If I am right about this, we need to agree how we respond to this deteriorating situation. The pessimists have already given their answer. Many of those who can are leaving Britain. Is it now a million who have already sold up and are ensconced in Spain? Similar numbers are buying properties there and in France and farther afield, so that one day they can leave their mother country. Other pessimists who stay seek what protection they can from enclosed estates, the employment of private security companies and a newly found faith in the CCTV camera which puts the simple hope of the medieval pilgrim to shame.

I do not yet share that pessimism. But hope is only a rational response to events if our politics change to reflect what should be the agenda. If we sweep back to ancient Greek and Roman politics, the models to which most major politicians and political academics looked for guidance when shaping the franchise, we find an agenda dominated by a single question: what sort of people should we and our fellow citizens be?

The Victorians asked and answered that question. As importantly, they actively sought to ensure that civil society and the family would progressively deliver the type of citizens who would, in Geoffrey Elton's words, be conscious of one another, yet leave one another alone. As we move from the politics of class to the politics of behaviour, part of any successful counter-strategy is to look again at the ideas Eleanor and her small group of feminist supporters advocated to reshape a world which responds to the needs of women and children. This is far from a purely intellectual exercise. The full force and horror of collapsing behaviour now pushes us in this direction. In examining afresh Eleanor's second-stage agenda we shall, I believe, be looking at the flipside of how best to counter anti-social behaviour.

What might be done?

The government sees work as the antidote to many of the social problems inflicted upon us. It does so without ever conceding that when and how we work might be a cause of some of those very problems. To a large extent, the government is correct to reinforce the truth that it is work that helps the world go round. Work is also important in giving us independence and the dignity that goes with that, as well as, thankfully, providing access to a range of friendships that might not otherwise exist. But does a strategy of work, work and work again necessarily further the best interests of very young children?

At the moment most mothers with young children have to work, irrespective of what their emotions and instincts tell them. But the blaze of publicity that the government has given to recent research showing the beneficial effect of nursery education on children from the age of two years and beyond also highlights an agenda which the government is less willing to advance. The very same study shows that most children are best nurtured by one of their parents in the first two formative years of their lives. While some fathers have the skills to nurture, and while others might acquire such skills by great diligence, the truth is that the nurturing of their young is natural to most women. The debate therefore needs to pick up where Eleanor and Eva Hubback left it when their deaths in the early post-war years took them from the public stage. Indeed, to me it is quite clear that Eleanor was correct at the beginning of her campaigning life to talk of the 'endowment of motherhood'. I can understand the tactical reasons for the change in language. But once the name did change to 'family allowances', let alone 'child benefit', the crucial focus Eleanor gave to the importance of nurturing and motherhood was lost. Moreover, it defused the case for radically enhancing the position of women with young children.

But Eleanor would, I am sure, be the first to ask where the money is to come from to ensure that the reform leads to an endowment scheme worthy of that name. For the endowment scheme to provide mothers with young children with the real choice of caring and nurturing their children full-time, the endowment must be paid at a level equal to what most mothers can gain at work. To start a campaign for such an endowment without first suggesting which funds might be available to make effective a choice for mothers with young children holds an obvious danger. It could be seized upon as yet another stick with which to beat mothers, many of whom already feel guilty that they have been forced to return to work very early on in their child's life. But, as Eleanor so often demonstrated, skilful political footwork can minimize such dangers.

The government has already stated its intention to increase the length of time over which maternity pay can be drawn, so as to cover the first nine months of a child's life. It also is hinting at extending paternity leave. But no minister has spelt out how such a policy fits in with the wider agenda of shaping the kind of citizens we wish the next generation to be. It is, however, easy to see the attraction of endless statements on maternity and paternity leave. The cost falls largely on the employer. But if the employer is not to pay, then who will? And what about setting the statutory maternity pay at a decent level? Likewise, where might the money come for the remainder of that first year, as well as that crucial second year of a child's life?

One reform might be to consider whether a significant proportion of the total budget giving financial support to children up to the age of 16 might not be better spent concentrated during the first two years of a child's life. I asked the House of Commons Library what additional weekly income could go to mothers if a quarter of the current child benefit and child tax credit bill was paid to mothers during the first two years of their child's life, rather than, as at present, spread over a 16-year period. From these sums alone an endowment of £24,000 tax free could be paid to all mothers over the first two years of each child's life.[8]

I am not advocating that an endowment policy for mothers with young children should be paid in this way. I merely wish to illustrate what could be achieved from reallocating the existing financial support for children. Nor am I arguing that a policy of endowment should stand alone. It should be buttressed by much greater efforts to transmit between generations the skills of good parenting, and likewise teach more generally guidelines which affirm those verities which good families still continue to impart to their young, but to which we no longer universally adhere.

Parenting skills

Endowment by itself does not deal with the issue I am raising. Children also need the active support of two parents and, where possible, grandparents. Even though this may not be the norm for many families today, what is best for children should not be denied for the fear of offending a perceived political correctness. To state an obvious truth is not to attack those families who do not fit this pattern. It is rather to break into a conspiracy where our silence acts against what children have a right to expect in normal circumstances, which it is a duty of both parents to meet and which the whole of our society should support both financially and culturally.

The door to this debate is more open than some observers dare to hope or others to fear. I recently asked senior pupils in a secondary school in Birkenhead, and a similar group in Manchester, to draw up for me what they would like to see in their school contract. You may remember that the government requires parents, pupils and the school to sign such a contract. It was noticeable that only one of the pupils questioned could produce the contract that she had signed, and none of the pupils, including the one who had the contract tucked away at the back of her notebook, could recall reading any such document.

I asked them if they were drawing up their part of the contract – parents, teachers, governors and governments would also similarly be involved – regarding what they would most want to gain from their school. What surprised me was that their top requests were identical in both schools. The number one priority was for schools to become safer places and to reduce the amount of bullying. This result surely hints at an extent of bullying which is still too inadequately perceived by the outside world. Their second request was to learn skills so that they could make good friends. Their third request was to acquire skills which would interest a good employer. In both schools their fourth request, one which both shocked and delighted me, was that they wanted to be good parents.

How might we deliver this fourth objective? No education reform is going to be successful if politicians believe they can pile yet more duties on schools. I therefore asked the education officer in Wirral if I could meet a panel of teachers, heads and inspectors to work out how we might, within the existing national curriculum, respond to the request of those young pupils. We are currently looking, for example, at which novels could be set for English Literature GCSE which present a range of different models of parenthood. Likewise, in the biology syllabus, we will be looking at how humans and other animals nurture their young and the importance of this nurturing.

A contract society

How these reforms could be built into an effective school contract I have tried to detail elsewhere.[9] But there is more to changing behaviour than just this. Rituals, as well as contracts, have an important role to play in any society. As traditional rituals cease to hold our affections in the way they once did, I believe it important that we invent others to take their place, or to run alongside them. As just one example the building up of a school contract, where there are serious negotiations between the different parties, must be followed by a series of public ceremonies at the school, involving all three parties, where these contracts are signed. The aim of the ceremony is publicly to reinforce the importance of the contract and to win a commitment to it. I have made the case elsewhere for reinventing initiation ceremonies, making the registration of births take on the welcoming role to a society once played by a universal baptism policy. Likewise, there is a need for a secular language to universalize a coming-of-age ceremony to denote the move from childhood towards that of approaching the life of an adult.

Similarly, in order to emphasize the price of the entry ticket into society, the contract side of welfare now needs to be brought to the fore. It is already there in the national insurance system. It is totally lacking in the fast-burgeoning means-tested welfare of current governments.

The idea is to begin a national discussion on what society wants in return for footing the welfare bill. The welfare contract would be mutual. Individuals signing on for the first time would be told what their entitlements are; similarly, society would set out the duties of those receiving this income. The duties would merely list what most of us still regard as reasonable behaviour.

This exercise will be important for society as we will be coming together to affirm what we regard as the rules of behaviour, which those of us lucky enough were taught naturally in our families. The contracts would be a public declaration of what normal behaviour is. As such they would reassure most people that what their instincts tell them is what the public requires. For others it would set the necessary tramlines within which society expects them to set their behaviour.

Conclusion

I began by highlighting some of the many aspects of Eleanor Rathbone's greatness. I likewise hinted at the relevance of many of her views more than half a century after she died. Not only that, but I have taken one aspect of her feminist beliefs to suggest its importance to what voters rate as one of the most important domestic issues, namely the collapse of decent behaviour. Eleanor was very much a child of the Victorian age and, while she lived through two horrendous world wars, she never lost that optimism in progress which was such a characteristic of the Victorians. While she might well have been dismayed at the collapse in behaviour, she would have been optimistic about the future. What I have tried to suggest is that her original policy of endowing motherhood has more relevance to countering anti-social behaviour than might at first be thought. The seriousness of the situation forces us back to consider how important are the very first years of our lives in deciding what kind of people we will turn out to be. Eleanor would have been quick to harness the politics of behaviour to focus attention on the pivotal role of motherhood in producing the kind of citizens necessary for a peaceable kingdom. And she would have reinvigorated her political campaign to achieve that objective. The greatest tribute we could pay to her would be to do just that.

10

Looking back to greatness: 50 years on

————◦•◦•◦————

Why in 1996 should we have devoted time to commemorating the fiftieth anniversary of Eleanor Rathbone's death? It is not, I wish to suggest, simply because she was a Rathbone, even though that Liverpool merchant family has had such a profound and wholesome impact on Merseyside, part of which I am proud to represent. Nor is it, I suggest, because she developed her father's approach to social issues and used her research to draw nationwide conclusions. Nor does she deserve remembering simply because she bucked the party system, becoming elected first to Liverpool City Council, and then to the House of Commons, as an independent. Nor should we primarily remember her for that voyage she undertook on a 'boundless bottomless ocean', to use Oakeshott's phrase about political activity, with only her own moral code as map and compass, for that was a journey upon which so many people embarked in late Victoria times. Nor, dare I suggest, should she be remembered only as a feminist, although she was undoubtedly one of the most effective of their campaigners.

Claims to greatness

Any one of these distinctions could make Eleanor Rathbone an interesting twentieth-century figure. The combination, however, secures her a substantial place in this country's annals. Yet I intend to argue for her a higher place. On four different counts, Eleanor's life's work carves out a greatness which we should not simply remember but actively celebrate.

There is, first, her contribution to economic thought. The title of her great book, *The Disinherited Family*,[1] sums up the campaigning message she addressed to the wider audience. The idea of the 'family wage' was a misnomer. Large numbers of those drawing such a reward had no children, and many of those who did had so many that the family wage packet was still inadequate to meet family needs. Her attack on a wage system which so favoured men not surprisingly incurred the hostility of trade unions which were then, unlike now, predominantly male-orientated, but led to two further developments. Only by neutralizing the impact of children in wage negotiations could women hope to win the battle for equal pay. Here, Eleanor was instinctively wearing her feminist hat. Her attack went to the heart of the matter. She changed the debate about the distribution of income away from what she saw as an obsession with the distribution between classes and towards one centring on differences between those households with and without children. And, equally important, Eleanor was concerned about who got what within the family. This is a debate which has still to run its revolutionary course in Britain. But let no one underestimate the pioneering impact Eleanor had on our thinking. *The Disinherited Family* secures for her a place in twentieth-century economic classics, equal, I believe, to Keynes' *General Theory of Employment, Interest and Money*. In some passages her prose equals that of Keynes' scintillating style, and she manages to express herself in a way that makes algebraic equations redundant.

Eleanor's second claim to greatness stems from what she did with these ideas. It was her early thinking, provoked by her painstaking study of the lack of well-being among the families of Liverpool dockers and merchant seamen, which led first, in 1917, to the Family Endowment Committee and then, in 1924, to the Family Endowment Society. It was her campaigning activities through these organizations which resulted in major legislative change. Her research findings into the World War I separation allowances to service families pulled Eleanor in one direction only. Outgrowing her father's tradition of social reform – although such a statement needs to be very carefully qualified – Eleanor looked to legislative action to deal with an obvious social evil. And here Eleanor fits into that great British tradition of reform by association which registered its impact through the great nineteenth-century societies, but also builds a bridge to the twentieth-century model. The birth of the Disablement Income Group, the Child Poverty Action Group and Shelter in the 1960s was not so much an innovation in interest-group politics as a renewal of a long tradition with deep roots in British political culture. British politics have always been about the representation of interests. It was an approach within which Eleanor disinterestedly worked for the whole of her political life. Few opportunities for showing the relevance of family allowances were missed, even if such a range of frenetic activity could in some instances appear inconsistent. Much of this activity was conducted outside Parliament: in the press, before committees, through the Independent Labour Party and thereby the trade unions and the Trades Union Congress. In an act of generosity, of which the House of Commons is occasionally capable, ministers and Members alike paid rightful tribute to Eleanor at the completion of the Family Allowance Bill. It was a half-nurtured measure, but it nevertheless brought about a most profound change in fiscal and social policy. The living standards of children were to some extent to be decided upon by the nation as a whole, and were not any longer to be determined solely by the capriciousness of the market.

Eleanor's third claim to greatness is hinted at in that act of parliamentary generosity. She was, without question, one of the truly impressive parliamentarians of the twentieth century. In saying this I am not ignoring the insensitivity which she so often displayed, and which would leave ministers diving for cover as they spied her descending upon them in the corridor.

No, I am looking at something much more important. And it is partly revealed by the examination of the entries under her name in *Hansard*. Both the length of entries and the range of subject-matter are truly staggering and, for a current parliamentarian, somewhat shaming. There are, of course, some clear differences between then and now. Eleanor did not have a constituency to attend to in the normal sense of the term. She was returned by the Combined English Universities as the Member for one of the 12 university seats when Members were returned on the vote of graduates of those universities. There were no surgeries, no welfare officer functions which MPs, in an age of politically footloose voters, have embraced partly for the good reason of self-interest. But it would be fair to add that, both by the nature of her graduate electorate and by the sheer range of her activities, Eleanor generated much constituency work when most party MPs would have had precious little. It was therefore important that she had a substantial private income and could afford two private secretaries to help organize and work her day. She never had to consider the question of how to earn a living and combine this with a very public life. Why is it that so few biographers mention, let alone adequately deal with, this very important aspect of a person's freedom to operate in the public domain? Susan Pedersen's study is a wonderful exception and, in part, so revealing because this side of Eleanor's life changes a view about the warmth for her within at least part of her family. Roy Jenkins' *Gladstone* is another model exception here in the detail he provides of Gladstone's fluctuating financial affairs. Professor Simey, who wrote of Eleanor so perceptively and affectionately, is surely right when he questions the longer-term impact on the political system of the decline in public affairs of this leisured class.

Yet, when all the excuses have been given, her work still stands out, and not only through an index of topics. There is too the sheer quality of the work. Take, as one example, her evidence to the Royal Commission in the mining dispute. I have yet to read any of today's pressure-group submissions which are comparable in quality, and I say that as someone who has also drafted more than I care to remember. Through her own contribution she deserves a bracketing with Asquith, Churchill and Thatcher as a parliamentarian – certainly lacking Asquith's ability as 'the big hammer', to use Campbell-Bannerman's phrase of the latter's debating skills – undoubtedly missing Churchill's mastery of painting with words; and not at all diminished by failing to have Thatcher's ability to dominate. But her own combination of integrity, expertise, disinterestedness, passion, choice of subject, ability, sheer staying power and effort puts her at the top table of twentieth-century parliamentarians.

Eleanor's final claim to greatness stems from that choice of subject. She will be rightly celebrated today as a feminist. But it is not her feminism which wins for her the spurs of honour. It is the importance she gave to individuals – or perhaps I ought to say the individual – which I see as the great driving force to her feminism, and indeed everything she touched. She regarded each individual – at least if they were women and children – as sacred. Men she generally saw as having all too many powerful champions to attract much of her interest. But when life itself was threatened – as it was by the Nazis – even this distinction held no value. It must have been that all-powerful commitment to protecting the individual, as well as being wonderfully well-informed, that led Eleanor to warn the country, in much clearer terms than did Churchill, of the evils and dangers of the Hitler regime. By February 1934 her voice was raised against the Nazis' 'blood-stained hands'. There was for her no phoney rapprochement, which so many of the British elite went through before collapsing into appeasement to that wicked regime. And it was the sacredness of the individual which led her to be the chief of parliamentary champions for those Jews trying to escape the Hitlerite terror.

On one of my regular trips to the National Portrait Gallery I attempted to buy a postcard of Eleanor's portrait. There was no demand. No one could remember anyone asking for a copy. There was no request in the suggestions book that such a card should be produced. By 2008 the portrait itself had disappeared into the bowels of the gallery! What future is there for a country whose collective memory is so frail that one of the truly great twentieth-century figures should have already passed from our general consciousness? Is there not a lesson in the fact that it was the Holocaust Trust that organized the only memorial gathering to mark the 50-year anniversary of Eleanor's death, and to remember her for her fight against Nazism, and her championing of the oppressed in Central Europe? No doubt Eleanor and her lifelong friend Elizabeth Macadam might have allowed a wry smile to cross their public-spirited faces at the thought that, 50 years after death, it would be groups who also champion life's sacredness that strive to keep alive the whisper of Eleanor's greatness.

11

The whisper of greatness[1]

————◆·◆·◆————

At last Eleanor Rathbone has been appropriately matched. Susan Pedersen's outstanding biography places Rathbone where she should be: one of the outstanding backbench MPs over the last 200 years. Rathbone's record outstrips those of Cobden and Bright, the great campaigners for free trade. They, after all, swam with an incoming tide. And she ranks with William Wilberforce, the great slave emancipator, although he not only had advantages of birth, such as William Rathbone ensured for his daughter, but also had the distinct advantage of being a man reforming a man-made world. A standard biography was published by Mary Stocks a few years after Eleanor's death in 1946. But Pedersen refocuses the lens through which we see Rathbone, and in so doing changes the record in numerous ways, and in particular in three important respects.

Eleanor and Elizabeth Macadam

First is the relationship with her lifelong partner, Elizabeth Macadam. At Rathbone's death Elizabeth burned practically the whole of their mutual correspondence. In today's prurient times, Pedersen suggests that the wrong conclusion is likely to be drawn from such an action. Many unmarried women of Eleanor's age believed that they could not have both a career and marriage. They consciously sought a career in a man's world and an emotional satisfaction equal to that from marriage from the closest of friendships with another woman, so keeping them free from the subjection which they saw as an inevitable part of marriage.

Very significantly, one of the few letters between these two outstanding women which survived the great burning is quoted here to full effect. After World War I, Elizabeth was offered a senior post running the Joint Universities Council for Social Science. Its acceptance, however, entailed her moving from Liverpool to London. The letter, which Elizabeth preserved, makes it clear that Eleanor wished her partner to act in Elizabeth's best interest, which, significantly, she did. But Eleanor acted after the letter was sent. She followed Elizabeth to London, demonstrating to Pedersen's satisfaction that, while Elizabeth could quite possibly have survived without Eleanor, the opposite was not true.

So why were so many of the other letters burned and this one saved? At so many points in the text, Pedersen surprises by the sheer quality of her insights. The serpent was full of pride: not a pride to conceal a part of the relationship which never existed, but a professional pride in that, by being linked to her great partner, she would herself be eclipsed when the record was written. Elizabeth believed that she, too, had been more than a foot-soldier in establishing Britain's welfare state. Elizabeth, the senior partner in the friendship according to Pedersen, willingly destroyed the correspondence to prevent her public record being overwhelmed by the role she played as Rathbone's political 'wife'. She kept a key document that confirmed what most observers would probably have guessed anyway, that she, Elizabeth, was very much the senior partner on the emotional front.

Eleanor and marriage

It was Eleanor's abhorrence of any physical contact, let alone a sexual one, which Pedersen again turns to such effect, and here is the second significant change to the established record. By viewing women as free from any sexual drive, and any emotional attachment that marriage might hold, Eleanor was able to see more clearly than almost anyone else the role economic power played in such partnerships. Her asexuality allowed Rathbone's eyes to bear down like torchlights on the economic position of women within the family. Her first published study on Liverpool dock work helped lead the campaign to decasualize this work. Her study of the position of the wives of merchant seamen working away from home for any length of time resulted, thanks to her follow-up campaigns, in the docking of merchant seamen's wages which were then paid directly to the wives. But Eleanor pondered on how families functioned economically.

Rathbone attacked the idea held by most radicals and trade unionists alike that the wage system should produce a family wage to support two adults and five children. If all income above this minimum level were taxed at 100 per cent and the money redistributed, there would still be inadequate resources to pay a wage for everyone equal to the needs of a family with five children. And so Eleanor's analysis led to her greatest book and one which, as I said earlier (see p. 132), should be placed alongside J. M. Keynes' *General Theory of Employment, Interest and Money*. While Keynes was concerned with changing the way the world viewed macro-economic policy in order to conquer unemployment, Rathbone wrought an equally significant revolution in focusing at a micro level on what then happened to this employment income within families. Her campaign led, ultimately, to the establishment of universal child benefit.

Eleanor and wealth

Pedersen is equally informative on another love that dares not speak its name. Now that sex is an open season, wealth has become the forbidden subject. Not so with Pedersen, who makes a third major revision. Those reading the existing literature know that Eleanor's father was important to her as the only man to whom she was ever emotionally close. She wrote his biography and, in doing so, erased her siblings from the record as well as her mother, whose marriage was by any guesstimate an erotic affair. But Eleanor, deliberately or otherwise, cleared away the living so that she would be seen as the natural public heir to William Rathbone the Sixth's public life.

William left his beloved second wife a huge fortune and then divided another fortune among his children. By treating Eleanor equally with her male siblings William ensured that Eleanor had a substantial private income, but hardly substantial enough for financing what became part of Eleanor's public career as the combined universities' MP. This was an age when there were no MPs' staff allowances or travel expenses: nothing but a meagre salary. Yet Eleanor employed two secretaries and household staff to help her. How Eleanor would have fared without this support we can never know.

That the missing money came, and in abundance, from Elsie, an unmarried half-sister whose life was as different from Eleanor's as could be imagined, tells us much about both these two characters. The established view, that Eleanor was one-dimensional, shy and at the best a prickly character, needs some revision. That Elsie should demote her brothers by ranking her half-sister's achievements above their disappointing behaviour tells us something about the warmth of association which clearly flowed out of sight. As Pedersen makes plain, Eleanor's achievements were in part made possible by the judgement of her half-sister in ensuring that Eleanor possessed a very substantial private income for her political work.

Elsie's judgement was vindicated. Much of the income from this fortune was spent in financing the campaigns Eleanor helped to organize to save individuals caught by the Nazi and Franco tyrannies. From this point Eleanor ceases to be only a feminist. Within no time of Hitler stealing power to become chancellor in 1933, she and Churchill were warning of the grave consequences for Europe. She was one of the key players behind the scenes in the overthrow of Chamberlain and the assumption of the premiership by Churchill. She also played a fundamental part in organizing the rescue of European Jews.

Fifty years after her death, the Holocaust Trust brought together some of the children whose lives she had, with huge effort, freed from Hitler's grasp, and my address to that gathering was published as the previous chapter. There was no other public celebration of this outstanding person's life, apart from by those Jews who had not forgotten her greatness. Modestly, in Liverpool, in the university in whose establishment Eleanor's father had been such a prime mover, Susan Pedersen spoke movingly about her work in bringing knowledge of this great person home to her own city. The hope must be that, with a biography of such distinction, Eleanor's reputation will also be returned to an almost too absent-minded world, and that now, thanks to this beautifully written book, the whisper of her greatness will never cease to excite.

Part 4

LEADING THE MASTER CLASS

Introduction

Beveridge was the great welfare reformer. But he was much more than that. Each decade of his life was filled with success that most of us would be pleased to report as a lifetime achievement. He conceptualized the great evil of unemployment, proposed how it should be dealt with and, by helping administer his new scheme, put an indelible mark on the pre-World War I Liberal government's welfare reform programme. He did the same after World War II but on an even grander scale, and his child, now growing old, is one we easily recognize. He was a complicated and at times impossibly annoying individual. But, by setting out the social programme for the Attlee government, he earned himself the place as the great social reformer of the last century. This outstanding record makes him a suitable last entry into my portrait of figures touched by the finger of greatness.

12

Beveridge: in a league of his own

———•◦•———

Had Churchill died before his sixty-fifth birthday he would have certainly regarded his life as a failure. Yet life's fanfare for Churchill began early: he was a Cabinet Minister before he was 34. Then came the near disastrous Dardanelles Campaign during World War I, a less than impressive stewardship as Chancellor of the Exchequer, a total misjudgement of Edward VIII's infatuation with Mrs Simpson and an equally unsuccessful rearguard action against Indian Home Rule. Churchill did not become prime minister until he was 65, and the rest is a triumphant history.

The record looks very different for William Beveridge. Even had there been no great welfare state blueprint in the middle of the war, when Beveridge had already celebrated his sixty-second birthday, his life would still have been worthy of much celebration. So what sort of person was Beveridge? What made him tick, and what were the forces that so drove him that, at the very point of death, he shot up in bed and exclaimed, 'There is much work to do!' and then, typically, died very efficiently?

'The boy Beveridge'

The contrast with Churchill could not in fact have been greater. There is not a decade of Beveridge's life that did not record success that would cap most people's careers. Within four years of entering Balliol, Beveridge had won firsts in three great schools: classics, mathematics and law. As a 24-year-old,

Beveridge became deputy to Canon Barnett, the Warden of Toynbee Hall, and lived at the settlement, as did all the other middle- and upper-class volunteers. The Settlement Movement played a part for half a century or more, beginning in the 1880s, in developing radical politics and providing a serious introduction to the 'condition of the people' question for would-be politicians. No such comparable training is provided today on the scale of the Settlement Movement, which left hardly any English city untouched by its activities.

Beveridge, while finding Toynbee Hall less than ideal, benefited twice over from his contact with the good Canon. Barnett aimed to expose his young volunteers to the social problems of the poor and therefore continue the Idealist tradition that our governors should be properly trained before they began to carry out their duties in high office. But Barnett's 'greatest gift to Beveridge was to steer him in the direction of trying to come up with a solution to the problem of unemployment'.[1] While Beveridge was at Toynbee he became involved in the unemployment committees in London, giving out doles. Thankfully Beveridge found this work hugely unsatisfactory. He kept being drawn back to the question Barnett had set him to answer: what are the causes of unemployment and what should be done to prevent it?

Within a couple of years Beveridge was poached to become leader writer on the *Morning Post*. Here the paper's right-wing backer made no stipulation about how Beveridge should develop his arguments in the leader columns, only that he was to specialize in unemployment and all the other social issues about which Beveridge was anyway thinking and writing.

His editorials, together with his active involvement in committees on unemployment, gave him his first substantial political break: an introduction to Sidney and Beatrice Webb, the great Fabian reformers. While the Webbs differed substantially from Beveridge on how best to tackle unemployment, they valued thinkers who might disagree with them, and it was they who introduced Beveridge to Winston Churchill, then the coming politician. Churchill was about to follow Lloyd George as President of the Board of Trade in the great pre-World War I Liberal reforming government, and Churchill was intent, like Lloyd George before him, on making his name as a social reformer.

Beveridge met Churchill at the Webbs' house on 11 March 1908. Among the other guests was C. F. G. Masterman, whose career as a significant welfare reformer fell like Icarus when he was made a Cabinet Minister soon after the start of the First World War. Being appointed to the Cabinet then required MPs to resubmit themselves to their constituents in a by-election, and Masterman twice failed to win that by-election contest. But after this gathering Beveridge recorded Masterman's comment that, given Mrs Webb's zeal for disciplining people, he prayed, should he become unemployed, never to fall into her hands.[2] Masterman, as he descended into drink, did, in fact, become largely unemployable, but he remained quick-witted enough to escape the clutches of the indefatigable Mrs Webb.

Beveridge's career as a great social reformer was about to be launched into the political stratosphere. A few weeks after this first meeting at the Webbs' Churchill became President of the Board of Trade. The Webbs told Churchill that, if he was to deal with unemployment, he 'must have the boy Beveridge'.[3] Early in July Beveridge had his second meeting with Churchill when he was invited to a departmental seminar which Sidney Webb, Llewellyn Smith, the Permanent Secretary to the Board of Trade, and Churchill attended. Churchill and Beveridge argued over the merits of a voluntary or a collective system of labour exchanges. On leaving the meeting Churchill overheard Beveridge say that he was about to go to the United States. Churchill responded to the effect that he 'must not be allowed to go'.[4] On the following day Beveridge was invited to become a full-time official at the Board of Trade to work on the labour exchange reform.

This event reflects well on Churchill, who also was never afraid of an argument with officials – or with anyone else, come to that. But it provided Beveridge's entry into the centre where welfare reform was being planned, commissioned and executed. During the time Churchill was at the Board of Trade (he left to become Home Secretary in 1910) he shielded 'the boy Beveridge', who was in fact not that much younger than himself.

Here beginneth an extraordinary story of an unelected reformer who, as a civil servant, kept a high public profile and used that profile, and his other great abilities, to leave a clear mark on the shape and form of the pre-World War I Liberal government's welfare reform programme.

Let me pause and take stock of these ten years of Beveridge's adult life. He had taken three first class degrees and won a law fellowship with no duties other than drawing £120 annual income. Within six years of going to Toynbee Hall, Beveridge had, as Lord Salter observed,

> personally studied the evil he was trying to cure, in the London docks and in Germany. He had created an inner circle of supporting opinion by his leading articles in an influential daily paper. He had himself both established and directed the system he had advocated. He had then crowned his work by a classic book which was for many years to be a guide and teacher to all those interested, whether as practitioners or students, in the social innovation he had introduced.[5]

So, within six years of going to Toynbee Hall and still only 30 years of age, Beveridge had to his credit this fourfold reforming pedigree. As Lord Salter has recorded, this is a record that has never been 'equalled before or since by a social reformer'.[6]

Successes and limitations

Beveridge continued to notch up major successes as a civil servant. He had an operational responsibility for a nationwide system of labour exchanges. On to these exchanges he grafted the first of Britain's insurance benefits, in this instance a tightly drawn scheme for the most vulnerable workers. He moved to the Munitions Ministry, back to the Board of Trade, and then into a new Food Ministry of which, by 1919, he was made the Permanent Secretary. He twice crossed the trade unions, rightly I believe, in insisting on a quasi-military form of direction for key war workers and then again insisting, against trade union pressure, that war workers were covered by an extension to unemployment insurance. The unions waited to settle these particular scores.

After Churchill, his second mentor and protector in the early stages of his career was Llewellyn Smith, his chief at both the Board of Trade and the Munitions Ministry. Beveridge had shown himself to be a brilliant initiator of policy, but a downside to his character was only too apparent to those people called upon to work with him closely: he was a hopeless administrator when it came to managing people, and this severe limitation to his genius was only too apparent in his next big job.

Here the Webbs re-enter our picture. Beveridge accepted Sidney's offer to become the Director of the London School of Economics. Within the next 20 years Beveridge had transformed this small sickly child into the leading centre of social research in the country, and in the process reformed the University of London, of which the LSE was one of the constituent colleges, into a new centralized power in UK higher education. But at the LSE Beveridge's inability to work as part of a team was magnified many times over by his increasing intimacy with the person whom he appointed as the school's academic secretary, Mrs Janet Mair, the wife of his second cousin. During a long friendship with me, Barbara Wootton – who knew only too well the obstacles a man's world places in the way of women, including those with outstanding talents – expressed contempt for only two people, Janet Beveridge, as she became on her marriage to William in 1942, and Mrs Thatcher. There is something ironic that this feminist distaste was exclusively reserved for two upwardly mobile women. Perhaps it is easier to identify one's own faults in others similarly placed.

At the point at which Beveridge left the LSE in 1937 to become Master of University College, Oxford, many of the LSE staff expressed a similar feeling to that of cities liberated from a foreign invader. It was, however, from his Oxford base that Beveridge viewed his country's bleak future. War broke out in September 1939, at which point Beveridge believed, rather as the Kitchener recruiting poster of World War I proclaimed, that his country was greatly in need of his extraordinary talents. So why was there no call? Perhaps the major reason why Beveridge had not been invited back into Whitehall was that his personality went before him. By now Beveridge had built up a considerable reputation for being difficult, and more. Let me cite one witness who willingly subscribes to Beveridge's greatness.

In making a BBC *Analysis* programme on Beveridge, I used a recorded interview given by Harold Wilson who, before heading three Labour governments, had been in his early post-graduate days Beveridge's research assistant. Beveridge described Wilson as having a good head, being extremely methodical and being prepared to work extraordinarily hard. Wilson was less flattering about his boss when he was asked to describe what it was like working with the great man. Wilson replied, 'A bitch,' before going on to say,

> He was almost insufferable. You would put an idea to him, he would say go away and work it out…he hardly ever listened. He would sit there grunting which could have meant he was listening. You could tell when you had finished your little spiel that he hadn't…He was the rudest man I have ever met.[7]

The Beveridge Report

After considerable expenditure of effort, Beveridge in July 1940 finally got his foot back into the Whitehall door. His aim was to direct the whole of the nation's manpower or, in other words, to direct the war effort on the home front. Standing in his way was Ernest Bevin, the trade union leader whom Churchill had brought into his coalition government and who was, as Peter Hennessy described, the great political bulk carrier of this period.[8]

Among Bevin's extraordinary 'abilities' was one that allowed him to be a great hater, and he hated Beveridge. No doubt there had been meetings where Beveridge had played the superior Oxford tutor to the honest son of toil. But, as we have seen, Beveridge had also seriously crossed the trade union movement on two separate occasions while he was a power in Whitehall two decades earlier, and Ernie had a prodigious memory when it came to slights against the trade union movement, which he saw as contiguous with himself.[9]

Bevin was initially against a departmental review of social security benefits. Such a review became more pressing once the Royal Commission on Industrial Injuries closed down for the duration of the war. But any initial resistance Bevin had against a review was quickly overcome when he saw that here was an ideal departmental exit through which he could push Beveridge.

Beveridge wept when he learned of his fate. Far from master-minding war-time manpower, for which he had been writing a report, Beveridge was consigned to the Whitehall equivalent of Siberia with his appointment as Chairman of the Inter-Departmental Review Committee. But Beveridge did not cry for long.

Within a few days of his appointment, eyes now clear, Beveridge seized the opportunity he had unwittingly been offered. Within no time he had written the main headings of his report. Beveridge's approach was to find evidence to support his reforms, not evidence to shape the report. He had, of course, been socially observing for much of his life.

Beveridge used his evidence-gathering as a means, in part, of building bridges with past opponents, like the trade unions, whose dislike of him had been so profound towards the end of World War I that they blocked his appointment to the new Ministry of Labour, which seemed a department designed in heaven for his talents. But the evidence-gathering was also used to secure a coalition for the new world of which he was intent on being the architect. This blueprint was published in December 1942, to huge popular acclaim.

Although the report (*Social Insurance and Allied Services*) ran to 300 closely argued pages and was a sell-out for official publications, I wonder how many people ever read it. Despite numerous attempts, I have failed to read the report in its entirety. And while the report is billed by many commentators as being written in Bunyanesque language, I have found it singularly lacking in an appeal that I so wanted to find. Yet there are those phrases, like 'slaying' the five great giants, that the press used to push home Beveridge's message. In fact, what made this report was a combination of the timing of the publication and the media's role in building the report into a fast-emerging political agenda that centred on winning the people's peace.

I am running a little ahead of my story. Once it was realized in Whitehall how radical Beveridge's proposals were, forces were mobilized to postpone the report's publication. The resulting delay, however, worked wonderfully to Beveridge's advantage. Had the report not been held up but published to its original timetable, it might well have been lost in the welter of what seemed a never-ending catalogue of setbacks in fighting the war. As it was, the report was published a few days after Montgomery's success at El Alamein. It is at this point that the country's spirit began to rise. For the first time voters began to believe that, no matter how long the struggle would now take, victory for the Allies would in the end be assured. Beveridge's vision was seen as central to the way a victorious Britain would look.

It was this vision that the press projected, and it was the media who explained how war on the home front would commence. Central to this war would be the abolition of the five great social evils that had so scarred British industrial society –

idleness, ignorance, disease, squalor and want. While the details of Beveridge's scheme were devilishly complicated, the outline was wonderfully clear, not to say simple. The war had shown full employment was possible: it needed to be maintained. A national health service was required to abolish disease. The Butler Education Act would be on the statute book by 1944. A new physical world would be built and the buildings would reflect the basic needs of individuals to live in a community. 'Want', as Beveridge termed poverty, would be slain by a universal insurance scheme paid for by uniform weekly contributions which would gain the contributor a passport to equal value benefits in time of need.

Beveridge had been active on the publicity front long before his report was published. He had used the outstanding war-time production *Picture Post* to advertise how his talents were underemployed during his time under Ernest Bevin.[10] And, once his ideas were published, he was no sloth in promoting them. But he was more than ably assisted by the abilities of what today would be called a spin doctor in the form of Frank Pakenham, later known as Lord Longford. The report scooped the front pages on publication day. Overnight, a new prophetic figure had arisen with its straight hair, bird-like features and high-pitched meticulous Oxford voice.[11] 'The People's William' had been born by courtesy of Pathé News.

The government was caught off balance. Despite his earlier role in protecting the young Beveridge, Churchill would not meet Beveridge this time around. The Prime Minister's excuse for not engaging with the report was that his entire efforts were spent on winning the war. Churchill almost certainly knew that Britain would be seen to be brokenbacked financially as soon as the armistice was signed. Yet many MPs responded to Beveridge's proposals with huge and unabated enthusiasm, and the ensuing parliamentary debate resulted in the largest single vote against the coalition government during the whole of the war.[12] Beveridge's proposals were set to become part of the country's DNA.

A complicated package

And so Beveridge's reputation remains. Yet part of his attract-iveness, certainly for one who did not ever have to deal with him, was that he was undoubtedly a complicated package: com-plicated in terms of the ideas he promoted over his lifetime, and complicated in the way individuals perceived his relation-ship with fellow human beings. A good starting point for this aspect of Beveridge is to turn to the passages from Beatrice Webb's diary that Jose Harris cites at the start of her outstand-ing biography.

One year before the Second World War broke out, Beveridge went down to visit Sidney and Beatrice Webb at their home in Hampshire. Beatrice, as was her custom, went for a long walk with her guest, this time talking over those issues which had occupied their conversations for so much of the previous 30 years. On that evening Beatrice committed her observations to her diary:

> His [Beveridge's] conclusion is that the major if not the only remedy for unemployment is lower wages...if this does not happen the capitalists will take his money and his brains to other countries where labour is cheap...He admitted almost defiantly that he was not personally concerned with the condi-tion of the common people...He declared that he had no living philosophy – he was a thoroughgoing materialistic agnostic about man's relation to the universe; and he had no particular credo or ideal as to man's relation to man.[13]

Four years later Beveridge was one of the country's heroes and, as he modestly observed to Harold Wilson, 'from now on, Beveridge is not the name of a man: it is the name of a way of life, and not only for Britain, but the whole civilized world'.[14]

So many people have testified to the contrasting shafts in Beveridge's character. In a memorial lecture Harold Wilson, Labour premier in the 1960s and 1970s, remarked that Beveridge was 'probably the greatest administrative genius of this century' but added he was 'almost certainly the worst administrator'.[15]

Jose Harris sets out the chameleon-type image that Beveridge possessed, accepting that all the different views contain an element of truth and reflected 'what a baffling man' Beveridge was. There were those who proclaimed a dazzling intellect, but others equally well-placed who saw Beveridge as a crushing bore. Beveridge appeared to some witnesses as open and generous with his time, while others saw him as the high priest of self-centredness, not to say selfishness. There were those who led the 'People's William' movement, while others of equal distinction saw him as an authoritarian bureaucrat. Dame Mary Cox, a member of the Beveridge Committee and cited by Harris, records Beveridge as someone who would not give a blind beggar a penny. Yet it was the same Beveridge who gave away a third of his income to charities and to vulnerable family members.

This many-sided character appraisal is not to detract from Beveridge's greatness, nor should the citing of his views at various stages of his career be used to dismiss him as someone who was simply inconsistent. One of the real strengths of Beveridge's position, when he came to write his epoch-making report, was that he was able to draw on a number of political traditions which had interested him at some stage during his life. In his great report we see elements of what he learned at Toynbee Hall. It is clear, also, that while English Idealism did not capture him, there was 'undeniable' evidence of T. H. Green's influence. A more enduring influence was that of the social evolution which was much to the fore in Beveridge's formative years, when there was a widespread belief that Darwin's operation of the natural sciences needed to be transferred to the social sciences.[16]

So merely to cite one period of Beveridge's life and to argue that he was inconsistent, either before or later, is to misunderstand the man. Rather, it was one of Beveridge's outstanding strengths that he drew on most of his previous ideas when writing his great report. This report, for example, brought to the fore Beveridge's position on citizenship, a form of civic republicanism as Jose Harris observes, which linked into his much wider understanding of how healthy democracies need to function through civil society.

A final comment on Beveridge's legacy. I do not wish simply to stress how the framework within which welfare is delivered in this country still carries Beveridge's hallmarks. If he was alive today he would be very critical, as he was in later public debate, over how his welfare revolution turned out in practice. But as well as setting a framework for benefit delivery, Beveridge continues to dominate the intellectual debate. On the Sunday during which the final draft of my Welfare Reform Green Paper was being agreed, a small staff was gathered in No. 10 around Jeremy Heywood, already then one of the outstanding civil servants of his age. The Prime Minister was in Chequers, and from there he sent a draft preface for the Green Paper which included the over-generous comment that he viewed me as his Beveridge. This draft went to Peter Mandelson, who was also absent from the room, and when the document went to press that phrase had been struck out. That prime ministerial comment spelt out the power that Beveridge still holds when welfare reformers gather together, and its striking out can now been seen as a proper action by a government that has still seriously to embrace welfare reform.

Notes

Six heroes and one hymn sheet

1 Details of Green's funeral suggest that his wife, at least, wished to present Green as well within the Victorian broad-church tradition, and there is no evidence that she was being untrue to the way Green perceived his own views; J. Preste, 'The Death and Funeral of T. H. Green', *Balliol Record* (1998), pp. 23–6.

2 Michael Ramsey, at one time Archbishop of Canterbury, who disputes the influence of Idealism on the young Anglo-Catholic wing of the Church, nevertheless wrote that 'if it be held that Green's strength lay less in metaphysics than in social ethics, it is clear that he so presented metaphysics as to make religion and ethics inseparable'; A. M. Ramsey, *From Gore to Temple* (London: Longman, 1960), p. 10.

3 Quentin Skinner's lecture 'The Lost Liberty of the English Revolution', given at the British Library on 11 February 2009.

4 Cited by Peter Saunders in Frank Field, *The Ethic of Respect: A leftwing cause* (St Leonards, NSW, Australia: Centre for Independent Studies, 2006).

5 See my introductory essay in Frank Field (ed.), *Attlee's Great Contemporaries* (London: Continuum, 2009).

6 This is included in a speech Frank Weston, the then Bishop of Zanzibar, made to the Anglo-Catholic Congress in 1923, entitled 'Our Present Duties', in *Report of the Anglo-Catholic Congress* (London: Society of SS Peter and Paul, 1923).

7 Susan Pedersen, *Eleanor Rathbone and the Politics of Conscience* (New Haven: Yale University Press, 2004), p. 322.

8 See the review Clement Attlee wrote of Lady Violet Bonham Carter's book on Churchill in Field (ed.), *Attlee's Great Contemporaries*.

1 Last of the great Victorians

1 A review of Peter Hinchliff's *Frederick Temple, Archbishop of Canterbury: A life* (Oxford: Clarendon Press, 1998).

2 Simon Green, 'Archbishop Frederick Temple on Meritocracy, Liberal Education and the Idea of a Clerisy', in Michael Bentley (ed.), *Public and Private Doctrine: Essays in British history presented to Maurice Cowling* (Cambridge: Cambridge University Press, 1993).

3 The Clarendon Commission, which sat between 1861 and 1864, proposed curriculum and governance changes that were carried into effect in the 1868 Public Schools Act.

2 Father and son: the relative abilities of Frederick and William Temple

1 Stephen Spencer's comment was made in the discussion following a paper I gave on William Temple. See Stephen Spencer, *William Temple: A calling to prophecy* (London: SPCK, 2001). Adrian Hastings disagrees with my judgement, referring to a father 'whom he venerated unstintingly but who seem[ed] never in the slightest to have intimidated him'; Adrian Hastings, 'William Temple', in Geoffrey Rowell (ed.), *The English Religious Tradition and the Genius of Anglicanism* (Oxford: Ikon, 1992), p. 211.

2 Ieuan Ellis, *Seven Against Christ* (Leiden: E. J. Brill, 1980), is the classic account of the book and its aftermath.

3 Peter Hinchliff, *Frederick Temple, Archbishop of Canterbury: A life* (Oxford: Clarendon Press, 1998), p. 130.

4 Adrian Hastings, 'William Temple', presents one of the few views of William which are not laudatory.

5 John Kent, *William Temple: Church, state and society in Britain, 1880–1950* (Cambridge: Cambridge University Press, 1992).

6 George Bell in his life of Archbishop Davidson failed to do justice to this event, which is as revealing on Temple as it is on his successor; see G. K. A. Bell, *Randall Davidson, Archbishop of Canterbury* (Oxford: Oxford University Press, 1938), vol. 2, pp. 292–9.

7 Recently the Church Commissioners, who had taken the freehold rights of archbishops and bishops in lieu of a stipend, tried to

regain the park for development. They failed, partly because the campaign made much of why Frederick gave the gift in the first place.

8 E. R. Norman, *Church and Society in England 1770–1970* (Oxford: Clarendon Press, 1976), p. 180.

9 Simon Green, 'Archbishop Frederick Temple on Meritocracy, Liberal Education and the Idea of a Clerisy', in Michael Bentley (ed.), *Public and Private Doctrine: Essays in British history presented to Maurice Cowling* (Cambridge: Cambridge University Press, 1993).

10 For a good example here see F. B. Macnutt (ed.), *The Church in the Furnace* (London: Macmillan, 1918).

11 The best study of this aspect of Temple's life is Kent, *William Temple*.

12 A short account of the Life and Liberty campaigns is to be found in F. A. Iremonger, *William Temple, Archbishop of Canterbury: His life and letters* (Oxford: Oxford University Press, 1948).

13 Kent, *William Temple*, p. 116, views the series of books produced for the conference as of greater value than the conference itself. Nothing quite like them has appeared since.

14 Temple clearly helped shape the Butler 1944 Education Act. Temple was so beguiled by his own talk on the national role of the established Church in the nation's life, and thereby its schools, that the trust was largely betrayed in defending the independence of church schools.

15 Quoted in Alan M. Suggate, *William Temple and Christian Social Ethics Today* (Edinburgh: T. & T. Clark, 1987), p. 15. See also the valuable biographical introduction by Wilfred Richmond to Henry Scott Holland's *The Philosophy of the Fourth Gospel* (London: John Murray, 1920), pp. 9–12.

16 Frank Field, 'Political Culture: Renegotiating the Post-war Social Contract', in B. S. Markesinis (ed.), *The British Contribution to the Europe of the Twenty-First Century* (Oxford: Hart, 2002).

17 Peter Hennessy, *Never Again: Britain 1945–1951* (London: Jonathan Cape, 1992).

3 William Temple's business ethics: stymieing the left for a generation

1 F. A. Iremonger, *William Temple, Archbishop of Canterbury: His life and letters* (Oxford: Oxford University Press, 1950 impression).
2 Owen Chadwick, *Michael Ramsey: A life* (Oxford: Clarendon Press, 1990), p. 118.
3 E. R. Norman, *Church and Society in England 1770–1970* (Oxford: Clarendon Press, 1976), p. 180.
4 Norman Sykes, *The Church and State in England in the Eighteenth Century* (Cambridge: Cambridge University Press, 1934).
5 Cited in Iremonger, *William Temple*, p. 439.
6 Norman, *Church and Society in England*, p. 168.
7 John D. Carmichael and Harold S. Goodwin, *William Temple's Political Legacy: A critical assessment* (York: Mowbray, 1963), p. 17.
8 Carmichael and Goodwin, *William Temple's Political Legacy*, p. 19.
9 Carmichael and Goodwin, *William Temple's Political Legacy*, p. 20.
10 See Noel Annan's essay in J. H. Plumb (ed.), *Studies in Social History* (London: Longmans Green, 1955).
11 Cited in Norman, *Church and Society in England*, p. 238.
12 John Oliver, *The Church and Social Order* (York: Mowbray, 1968).
13 *Christianity and Industrial Problems* (London: SPCK, 1918), p. 80.
14 William Temple, *The Kingdom of God* (London: Macmillan, 1912), pp. 96–7.
15 William Temple, *Christianity and Social Order* (Harmondsworth: Penguin, 1942), p. 58.
16 Iremonger, *William Temple*, p. 578.
17 Iremonger, *William Temple*, p. 579.
18 Norman, *Church and Society in England*, p. 14.

4 William Temple: a political evaluation

1 Paul Addison, *The Road to 1945* (London: Jonathan Cape, 1975).

2 John Kent, *William Temple: Church, state and society in Britain, 1880–1950* (Cambridge: Cambridge University Press, 1992). An equally thoughtful read is Adrian Hastings' 'William Temple', in Geoffrey Rowell (ed.), *The English Religious Tradition and the Genius of Anglicanism* (Oxford: Ikon, 1992). The standard life is F. A. Iremonger, *William Temple, Archbishop of Canterbury: His life and letters* (Oxford: Oxford University Press, 1948).

3 Kent, *William Temple*.

4 Kent, *William Temple*, p. 116.

5 Headlam was lucky with his biographer; see Ronald C. D. Jasper, *Arthur Cayley Headlam: Life and letters of a bishop* (London: Faith Press, 1960).

6 Hastings, 'William Temple', p. 217.

7 Adrian Hastings, *A History of English Christianity, 1920–1985* (London: Collins, 1986), p. 217.

5 *Christianity and Social Order*: the book and the nation

1 F. A. Iremonger, *William Temple, Archbishop of Canterbury: His life and letters* (Oxford: Oxford University Press, 1948), p. 37.

2 Iremonger, *William Temple*, p. 41.

3 Joseph Fletcher, *William Temple* (New York: Seabury Press, 1963).

4 William Temple, *Christianity and Social Order* (London: SCM, 1950), pp. 49–50.

5 Temple, *Christianity and Social Order*, p. 50.

6 Temple, *Christianity and Social Order*, p. 57.

7 Cited in Stephen Spencer, 'William Temple's *Christianity and Social Order* after Fifty Years', *Theology*, vol. XCV, no. 763 (1992), p. 35. A much fuller consideration of Temple's ideas is to be found in Stephen Spencer, *William Temple: A calling to prophecy* (London: SPCK, 2001).

8 Cited in Spencer, 'Fifty Years', p. 35.

9 Cited in Spencer, 'Fifty Years', p. 35.

10 Cited in Spencer, 'Fifty Years', p. 36.

11 Temple, *Christianity and Social Order*, p. 62.
12 Maurice G. Tuckner, *John Neville Figgis* (London: SPCK, 1950).
13 Temple, *Christianity and Social Order*, p. 63.
14 Temple, *Christianity and Social Order*, p. 68.
15 Temple, *Christianity and Social Order*, p. 70.
16 G. K. A. Bell, *Christianity and World Order* (Harmondsworth: Penguin, 1940).
17 *Christian Faith and the Common Life* (London: George Allen & Unwin, 1938).
18 Adrian Hastings, 'William Temple', in Geoffrey Rowell (ed.), *The English Religious Tradition and the Genius of Anglicanism* (Oxford: Ikon, 1992), p. 244.
19 William Temple, 'Theology Today', *Theology*, vol. 39, no. 233 (November 1939).
20 Hastings, 'William Temple', p. 224.
21 See Dorothy Emmet's chapter in Iremonger, *William Temple*, in which she cites Temple's letter to her, pp. 537–8.
22 Barbara Robb, *Sans Everything* (London: Nelson, 1967).

6 George Bell: a uniquely consistent life

1 Anyone studying Bell is indebted to Melanie Barber, who was, when I gave this talk, the deputy librarian and archivist at Lambeth Palace Library, for the way she unselfishly puts her unrivalled knowledge of the Bell papers at an enquirer's disposal, and to the work in particular of Andrew Chandler.
2 Interview with Mary Joice, 14 October, 1991.
3 Ronald Jasper, *Arthur Cayley Headlam* (London: Faith Press, 1960).
4 Gordon Rupp, *I Seek My Brethren: Bishop Bell and the German churches* (London: Epworth Press, 1975), footnote 19.
5 See Donald Watt, 'The Historiography of Appeasement', in Alan Sked and Chris Cook (eds), *Crisis and Controversy: Essays in honour of A. J. P. Taylor* (London: Macmillan, 1976).
6 In Ronald C. J. Jasper, *George Bell: Bishop of Chichester* (Oxford: Oxford University Press, 1967), pp. 30–1.
7 Bell's introduction to his *The War and the Kingdom of God* (London: Longmans, Green & Co., 1915), p. 5.

8 One of the clearest understandings, and an illustration of the error most of his compatriots were making, is to be found in R. H. S. Crossman, 'From U-Boat to Pulpit', *Spectator*, 23 November 1934.

9 Cited in M. Daphne Hampson's fine work which, sadly, remains unpublished: 'The British Response to the German Church Struggles, 1933–1939', PhD thesis, University of Oxford, 1973, p. 145.

10 See his *The Economic Consequences of the Peace*, published in 1919 (New York: Harcourt, Brace and Howe). The details of past reparations come from the House of Commons Library Note, 9 January 2009.

11 Bell himself gives a brilliant insight into the workings of the Edwardian Constitution of those chapters which deal with 1903 to 1914 in his *Randall Davidson, Archbishop of Canterbury* (Oxford: Oxford University Press, 1935), vol. 1.

12 Lang commented on a portrait of himself painted by Sir William Orpen by observing, 'They say in that portrait I look proud, prelatical and pompous.' Hensley Henson heard this comment and quickly rejoined, 'And may I ask Your Grace to which of these epithets your Grace takes exception?' In J. C. Lockhart, *Cosmo Gordon Lang* (London: Hodder and Stoughton, 1949), p. 290.

13 Andrew Chandler, 'The Church of England and the Obliteration Bombing of Germany in the Second World War', *The English Historical Review*, vol. 108 (October 1993), pp. 930–1.

14 The most devastating comment of Bell as a speaker of 'almost overpowering dullness' comes in Kenneth Slack's *George Bell* (London: SCM, 1971), p. 116.

15 Bell's speech in the House of Lords *Hansard* is reproduced in his *The Church and Humanity, 1939–1946* (London: Longman, 1946).

16 Included in Bell, *The Church and Humanity*.

17 Interview by the author with the Rt Reverend James Herbert Lloyd Morrell, 8 January, 1992 (see pp. 79–80).

18 See, for example, Charles Smyth, *Cyril Foster Garbett* (London: Hodder and Stoughton, 1959), pp. 294–5.

19 See Hampson, 'The British Response', p. 174.

20 John Rawls, 'Justice as Fairness', in Peter Laslett and W. G. Runciman (eds), *Politics, Philosophy and Society* (Oxford: Basil Blackwell, 1962).

7 Piety and Provocation: A study of George Bell

1 Andrew Chandler, *Piety and Provocation: A study of George Bell* (Chichester: George Bell Institute, 2008).

2 Andrew Chandler, *The Church of England and the Twentieth Century: The Church Commissioners and the politics of reform, 1948–1998* (Woodbridge: Boydell Press, 2006).

9 Citizenship and the politics of behaviour: lessons from Eleanor Rathbone's thought

1 Publication of Susan Pedersen's masterful biography, which excels on so many fronts, will hopefully mark a decisive turn of the tide. See her *Eleanor Rathbone and the Politics of Conscience* (New Haven: Yale University Press, 2004). But *Eleanor Rathbone* (New York: Sage, 1996) by Joanne Alberti is a fine shorter study. Mary Stocks's *Eleanor Rathbone* (London: Gollancz, 1949) is valuable not least in the way it captures how Eleanor impacted on the lives of her close collaborators.

2 Sir Geoffrey Elton lived in a number of European countries before immigrating to Britain. This inaugural lecture at Cambridge was given in 1984, and is cited in Peter Hennessy, *Never Again: Britain 1945–1951* (London: Jonathan Cape, 1992), p. ix.

3 For the impact of the Evangelical Revival, two works are as important as they are illuminating. The first is Noel Annan's *Leslie Stephen* (London: Weidenfeld and Nicolson, 1984). The second is *Age of Atonement* by Boyd Hilton (Oxford: Clarendon Press, 1988).

4 This idea is richly developed, as one would expect, by Jose Harris. In particular, see her *Private Lives and Public Spirit* (Oxford: Oxford University Press, 1993), Ch. 8, and 'Political Thought and the Welfare State 1870–1940: an intellectual framework for British social policy', *Past and Present*, vol. 135 (1992), pp. 116–41.

5 The most informative single essay I have read on T. H. Green is by John MacCann in his *Six Radical Thinkers* (originally published 1910, reprinted New York: Russell and Russell, 1964). MacCann was Professor of Philosophy at Liverpool University, which Eleanor's father had been a key force in founding. The outstanding fuller study is Andrew Vincent and Raymond Plant, *Philosophy, Politics and Citizenship* (Oxford: Basil Blackwell, 1984).

6 Pedersen, *Eleanor Rathbone*, p. 191.

7 There is no adequate political life of Eva Hubback, although her daughter, Diana Hopkinson, published a largely affectionate study in *Family Inheritance: A life of Eva Hubback* (London: Staples Press, 1954). She ranks less than a page in the *Oxford Dictionary of National Biography* which is particularly surprising given that the *Dictionary*'s second editor, Brian Harrison, grasps her importance in an essay in his *Prudent Revolutionaries: Portraits of British feminists between the wars* (Oxford: Clarendon Press, 1987).

8 A note from the statistical section of the House of Commons Library, 6 December 2004.

9 Frank Field, *Neighbours from Hell: The politics of behaviour* (London: Politicos, 2003).

10 Looking back to greatness: 50 years on

1 (London: Edward Arnold, 1924).

11 The whisper of greatness

1 Susan Pedersen, *Eleanor Rathbone and the Politics of Conscience* (New Haven: Yale University Press, 2004).

12 Beveridge: in a league of his own

1 Helen Meller, 'Beveridge: The Early Years, English Culture and the Context for Social Policy Making', in W. John Morgan (ed.), *The Beveridge Plan 1942–1992: Fifty years on* (Nottingham: Institute of Modern Cultural Studies, 1994), p. 10.

2 Editorial note in *The Diary of Beatrice Webb*, vol. 3, edited by Norman and Jeanne Mackenzie (London: Virago, 1984), p. 90.

3 William Beveridge, *Power and Influence* (London: Hodder and Stoughton, 1953), p. 68.

4 Cited in J. Harris, *William Beveridge* (Oxford: Clarendon Press, 1977), p. 140.
5 Lord Salter, 'Lord Beveridge', *Proceedings of the British Academy*, vol. 44 (1963), p. 420.
6 Lord Salter, 'Lord Beveridge'.
7 *Analysis*, 30 November 2002.
8 See his essays in Frank Field (ed.), *Attlee's Great Contemporaries* (London: Continuum, 2009).
9 Field (ed.), *Attlee's Great Contemporaries*.
10 'Beveridge, the Man-Power Expert, is being Wasted Himself', *Picture Post*, 7 March 1942.
11 J. Harris, 'William Henry Beveridge', in H. C. G. Matthew and Brian Harrison (eds), *Oxford Dictionary of National Biography* (Oxford: Oxford University Press, 2004), p. 594.
12 Derek Fraser, *The Welfare State* (Stroud: Sutton Publishing, 2000), p. 78. The government was defeated on an equal pay vote for teachers, but this defeat was reversed the next day.
13 Harris, *William Beveridge*, p. 1.
14 Fraser, *The Welfare State*, p. 2.
15 Harold Wilson, *Beveridge Memorial Lecture* (London: Institute of Statisticians, 1966), p. 7.
16 Harris, *William Beveridge*, p. 2.